Coordinating Child Sexual Abuse Services in Rural Communities

Coordinating Child Sexual Abuse Services in Rural Communities

Barry Trute, Elizabeth Adkins, and George MacDonald

in association with

Kathryn McCannell and Carol Herbert

UNIVERSITY OF TORONTO PRESS
Toronto Buffalo London

© University of Toronto Press Incorporated 1994
Toronto Buffalo London
Printed in Canada

ISBN 0-8020-2999-X (cloth)
ISBN 0-8020-7450-2 (paper)

Printed on acid-free paper

Canadian Cataloguing in Publication Data

Trute, Barry, 1944–
Coordinating child sexual abuse services in
rural communities

Includes bibliographical references and index.
ISBN 0-8020-2999-X (bound)   ISBN 0-8020-7450-2 (pbk.)

1. Manitoba Rural Child Sexual Abuse Project.
2. Sexually abused children – Services for –
Manitoba – Case studies.   3. Sexually abused
children – Services for – Canada.   4. Rural children –
Services for – Manitoba – Case studies.   5. Rural
children – Services for – Canada.   I. Adkins,
Margaret Elizabeth.   II. MacDonald, George, 1949–   .
III. Title.

HV745.M36T78 1994   362.7'68'097127   C94-930335-6

University of Toronto Press acknowledges the financial assistance to its
publishing program of the Canada Council and the Ontario Arts
Council.

This book is dedicated to Elizabeth Hill.

Elizabeth Hill was an outstanding teacher, a skilled community advocate, and a respected clinician.

Her dedication to disadvantaged children and their families was nothing short of remarkable. When Elizabeth worked with a child, she worked with more than just a young person. She worked with the child, the child's family, and the child's surrounding social environment.

She was a natural healer. She was one of those rare individuals who could both politically empower and psychologically strengthen those with whom she worked.

Contents

Acknowledgments

This was a lengthy project that involved two years of preparation, three years of formal data-gathering and analysis, and two years of thoughtful reflection and writing. It was a project that involved the support of a network of consultants across Canada, the tenacious commitment of a research team, the loyalty and goodwill of many professionals practising in a wide range of human service agencies, and the patience and participation of many families at a chaotic and painful time in their lives. It is not possible to identify and thank each of the many people who contributed to the project upon which this book is based. However we do wish to acknowledge those who made a significant contribution to the overall effort.

Members of the core research team included Drs. Elizabeth Adkins and Barry Trute, acting as co-principal investigators. George MacDonald was project coordinator. Allison Cranmer, project secretary, was an essential assistant who maintained our research office and kept a watchful eye on the administration of our research grant. The research effort involved many student research assistants, several of whom gave us committed service over a number of years. Gloria Vaughan-Jones, Barbara Scuse, Kelly Scott, and Mary Anne Hildebrand deserve special recognition for their outstanding efforts.

Drs. Kathryn McCannell and Carol Herbert of the University of British Columbia served a co-investigators and were regularly available as research and practice consultants. As well, they played an active part in the design of the study, provided ongoing advice as research consultants, and participated directly in the community surveys conducted at the end of the service delivery phase of the project. Dr. Elizabeth Hill was involved in the project's early phases as a co-investigator. Dr. David Scuse acted as a co-investigator and computer consultant during the course of the project, and provided valuable technical consultation and research advice as well.

Although he was not a member of our research team, Dr. Robin Krause, in family medicine at the University of Manitoba, performed an important service as our liaison with physicians in southern Manitoba who participated in the study. Drs. Charles Ferguson and Carol Herbert provided important training modules to physicians participating in the project, to encourage and strengthen their involvement with the medical aspects of the investigation of child sexual abuse.

This project could have not been conducted without the support of National Welfare Grants of Health and Welfare Canada. It provided us with a research grant (Project # 4556-1-19) and with helpful advisors, including Robert Hart, David Allen, and Fran McIninch. With the assistance of National Welfare Grants, a national advisory committee (NAC) was created to provide research advice and guidance. Members of the NAC included skilled researcher-clinicians, Drs. Jane Bradley, Charles Ferguson, Gary Grams, and Dan Offord; representatives from the Province of Manitoba, Judge John Guy and John Chudzik; and representatives of the two participating child welfare agencies, Dennis Schellenberg, who served as chairperson of the NAC, and Murray Bergman.

The support of the Child and Family Services Research Group, the Faculty of Social Work, and the Psychological Service Centre, all within the University of Manitoba, is gratefully acknowledged.

The South Team of Child and Family Services of Central Manitoba (Dennis Schellenberg, Executive Director) functioned as the test or intervention site in the project. Investigation and treatment services were provided by Audrey Armstrong, Diane deLucia, Kathryn Levine, Harry Nott, Debbie Shannon, Bill Warren, Pat Armstrong, and Ken Sawatsky. Legal counsel was provided by Barney Christianson, Q.C. Treatment Services within the test community involved Community Mental Health Services (Tracy Fedoruk, Ron Laverty, Brenda Muirhead, Norma Tessier), the Eden Mental Health Centre (Kurt Guenther, Guido Farelli, Daphne Andrews-Peers, Heather Corbett, Kathie Genoway, Walter Wiebe), Family Services (Eleanor Chornoboy, Maria Owens), Corrections (Mel Armstrong, Frank Dabbs, Ken Waltman), Community Physicians (Drs. Dieter

Bueddefeld, Barbara Perkins, Connie Woelk), and the Committee on Family Violence (Donna Rosling-Wolters, Carol Smith). The involvement of the RCMP was facilitated through the thoughtful efforts of Inspector Ian Parsons, Corporal Russ Waugh, and Staff Sergeant Martin Kerelchuk.

The South Team of Child and Family Services of Eastern Manitoba (Dave Waters, Executive Director) functioned as the comparison or regular-services site in the project. Investigative services were provided by Bob Barry, Edith Fransen, Norman Hiebert, and Joanne Jeffries, with support services by Giselle Roche and Elvira Toews.

The most important participants in this project were the children and families who consented to our involvement in their lives. We are most grateful to them for sharing their experiences and views with us. They cannot be identified, but they are the ones who served as sources of the information that was so vitally important to this challenging research effort.

B.T.
E.A.
G.M.
Winnipeg, 1993

The Design and Implementation of Coordinated Community Services to Respond to Child Sexual Abuse

1

Introduction

Child Sexual Abuse: The Need for a Coordinated Service Response

A disclosure of incest or intra-familial child sexual abuse triggers a state of uncertainty in victims, alleged perpetrators, and their family members. It mobilizes professionals across a number of human service sectors. It is a crisis within the family because it exposes to the outside world a situation that in the past has been carefully shrouded in secrecy. It creates stress in networks of extended family and friends who have close social and emotional ties to the victim or to members of the immediate family. They are drawn into the problem, and are expected to protect and support members of a family that is now formally identified as 'incestuous' and that may be in a state of turmoil. It is a challenge to statutory human service agencies, such as child protection services and police, which must investigate allegations of child sexual abuse and prepare evidence for what might eventually be some combination of healing, protection, and punishment. It places complex demands on treatment providers. They must navigate resistance and denial, merge treatment priorities with protection concerns, and facilitate healing in what can be a multi-generational problem – a problem that often intertwines sexual behaviour, which can have addictive qualities, with coercive or violent behaviour against a child. This is a highly complex social problem that requires specialized investigative and treatment skills. It is a circumstance that demands careful multiagency coordination and thoughtful, integrated service interventions at the level of the person, the family, and the community.

Despite the obvious need, there is a dearth of services available to respond to this client population. Interventions that do exist tend to be sparse, sporadic, and piecemeal in approach, with no systematic follow-up or evaluation. Often, services are available to specific target clients (most usually the victim and perpetrator seen separately), with little consideration directed to other family members or to the social environment in which the abusive behaviour has occurred. Many vulnerable children and families fall between the cracks in existing service systems. These cracks are created, not only by the scarcity of service resources, but also by the confusion and lack of coordination among the services that do exist (Finkelhor, Gomes-Schwartz & Horowitz 1982; MacFarlane & Bulkley 1982). The Badgley Report (1984) notes how the response to the need for services for child sexual abuse has tended to be sporadic and uncoordinated in Canadian communities. It recommends that priority attention be given to service fragmentation and that there be 'more effective coordination of efforts between public agencies providing complementary services to sexually abused children' (p. 38).

One would anticipate that a service network, responding in a community to child sexual abuse, would logically welcome coordination of services and collaboration of effort. Child sexual abuse is widely recognized by human service professionals as a serious social problem that no one discipline or agency can handle adequately on its own. It seems obvious that the skills and mandates of different service sectors such as the police, child protection, and medical services all have an important and interdependent contribution to make in the response to child sexual abuse. Further, each discipline or agency needs the other to adequately fulfil its own basic service mission. These are interorganizational conditions that Litwak and Hylton (1962) suggest would create pressure and momentum for coordinated service delivery.

So why does service fragmentation persist in this field? Helfer and Schmidt (1976) identify administrative and political hurdles. They raise questions concerning the optimum governmental level at which services should be administered. They recognize the serious and malicious effects that interdisciplinary competitiveness, as well as agency protectionism of budgetary and program power, can have on integrated service responses. It seems that coordination or integration of services is 'primarily a consensus-building process' (Morrill 1976). However it is evident that such consensus building is not an easy proposition when it comes to the delivery of services that respond to child sexual abuse.

There has also been a recognition, by those more attuned to the clinical ramifications of child sexual abuse, of how challenging the treatment of these cases can be. Because of the powerful emotional issues linked to child sexual abuse, professionals can often be po-larized in their response, being pulled to be either advocates (for the victim, family, or perpetrator) or avengers (against the victim, family, or perpetrator). Those providing treatment services to fam-ilies in which incest has occurred are becoming more familiar with the systemic disruptions that these families can trigger in profes-sionals and between providers of treatment services. More persis-tent patterns of service disruption have been identified. These in-volve professionals coming to mirror the conflict within the troubled family system (Dale et al. 1986) or to act out conflicts on behalf of family members in what is termed 'conflicts by proxy' (Furniss 1983). These toxic service patterns usually correspond to conflict-avoiding manoeuvres within the family and, when viewed with some emotional distance (viz. from a 'meta-perspective'), can be seen as the failure of service providers to avoid being emotionally caught in the same dysfunctional patterns that plague the family they are struggling to assist (Furniss 1991). Disorganized families require the help of service systems that are not similarly disorganized if they are to find their own family solutions to vexing emotional problems.

Families have good reason to be on guard when facing a disclosure of child sexual abuse. At the time of the disclosure, two fundamental and identifiable crises are triggered by the allegation that there has been a sexual assault on a child. The first crisis is associated with a challenge to the stability of interpersonal relationships within the family, and the meaning the sexual abuse has in altering these re-lationships. Fundamental to this is the message that this is a family in which parents do not protect their children, and that the children are vulnerable to 'attack trauma' from within the family and cannot feel safe. This is a crisis based on an internal threat to family sta-bility. The second crisis is associated with external threats to the continued existence of the current family as it now exists. This oc-curs through the intrusion of what are often seen as hostile out-siders creating 'institutional trauma,' which has the potential to change the composition of the family. That is, they challenge the existing structures of family organization and control, or are responsible for the withdrawal or expulsion of one or more family members.

Despite the efforts of most professionals to provide safe and effective intervention and treatment, service-induced or 'institutional trauma' all too frequently occurs (Conte 1984; Giaretto 1976). This kind of trauma is again largely due to the predominant tendency of agencies in the human services to respond to sexual abuse in an isolated way, with a low level of interagency cooperation. Thus, the process of intervention often creates confusion and works against the goals of protecting the child, laying appropriate charges against the offender, and initiating treatment for the child, the offender, and family members. Both clients and service providers are usually left feeling frustrated, angry, and alone. Herbert, Grams, and Trute (1986) describe family members in situations of incest as 'feeling "suspended"; unclear of what will happen next, who will be involved, what they are to do, and how to understand the process they are involved in. By the time they get into therapy they are often feeling angry or have lost hope' (p. 5). Investigative and early treatment services, then, have become an iatrogenic influence, compounding the social and psychological damage to all members of families in which there have been allegations of incest.

A disclosure of child sexual abuse often initiates a complex response from agencies responsible for the protection of children and the maintenance of law and order in the community. Many human service sectors spanning child welfare agencies, police, medical services, mental health centres, and crisis centres claim some jurisdiction in the field of child sexual abuse. Child welfare agencies and police are directed by government legislation to investigate any allegation of assault on a child. Often, treatment services that could ameliorate the trauma associated with child sexual abuse are delayed, pending confirmation within the criminal justice system that the allegation of abuse is substantiated. Because of the complexity of such situations, the investigative process can be lengthy, confusing, and an extremely difficult time for victims and their families.

Professionals, who have different priorities and perspectives, and specific responsibilities for conducting different aspects of the investigation of alleged child sexual abuse, can often work at cross-purposes. Child welfare personnel are mandated to protect the physical safety and psychological well-being of the child. Police are mandated to investigate violations of the law and to ensure that adequate evidence is collected to meet the needs of the criminal justice system. These two mandates can create a powerful intrusion into the life of children and their families when different professionals make enquiries in a repetitive, and seemingly uncoordinated, manner. Outsiders asking many questions are seen to invade the life of the family. For victims there may be multiple interrogations that can serve to weaken their resolve to provide evidence, and that make them feel more vulnerable as family tension increases. It has been suggested that a 'child sexual abuse accommodation syndrome' (Summit 1983) often occurs, which leads children to retract disclosures as a way of coping with others' disbelief and lack of emotional support. For some children, the trauma associated with the investigative process can be more acute than the trauma of the sexual abuse that triggered the involvement of outsiders in the life of the family (Schultz 1973). A key element here is family dismemberment, which can be particularly poignant when children are removed from their homes to ensure their protection and safety.

MacFarlane and Bulkley (1982) offer a useful review of key patterns in the specific organizational relationship between child sexual abuse treatment programs and the criminal or juvenile justice systems. These include (1) the 'victim advocacy model,' which is highly victim-centred and promotes strong legal sanctions against those who perpetrate sexual abuse on children; (2) the 'improvement model' which, while maintaining a victim-centred orientation, pushes for more sensitive responses from the criminal justice system and seeks more success in securing prosecutions and guilty pleas; (3) the 'system modification model,' which seeks a major overhaul across entire legal systems in order to reduce trauma to children and families, and attempts to coordinate legal intervention with family treatment; (4) the 'independent model,' in which specialized treatment centres attempt to provide service with as much independence from legal proceedings as possible, but which do serve as expert consultants to the courts when their expertise is required; and (5) the 'system alternative model,' in which a treatment program maintains distance from the punitive functions of the criminal justice system and seeks to promote positive family change without coercion or force but through a trusting alliance with its clients.

Each of these approaches, in negotiating the community interface between courts and treatment providers, will have inherent strengths and weaknesses. It seems clear that when different treatment agencies in the same community hold competing ideologies regarding the relationship between the courts and treatment services, response from the courts will be inconsistent, thus blocking successful collaborative efforts on the part of key community treatment services that attempt, each in their own way, to respond to child sexual abuse.

An allegation of intrafamilial abuse, or assault by a trusted adult in the life of a child (such as a babysitter or family friend), creates a serious crisis that unbalances and threatens the internal stability of a family. In many instances, because of the serious ramifications of the situation, family members are slow to believe the victim. At times, the alleged perpetrator is protected for fear of family disintegration. Unfortunately, within the Canadian judicial system, most victims and their non-offending parents are left in a state of legal limbo while the investigation process is conducted. Often mental health treatment is withheld as well, pending the disposition of investigative findings. In the short term, too few children and their families receive family-focused counselling, help with key intimate relationships in their life, or help in coping with the social and psychological consequences of the disclosure of sexual abuse. If litigation seems imminent, many parents will protect their legal position, and what they see as their family's best interests, by curtailing discussion of the abuse situation – particularly with professionals who are attempting to provide early treatment services.

This is a lost opportunity for those who can help the family to heal – that is, the opportunity to enter into the life of the family when its members are in crisis and their defenses lowered. People in crisis are often more psychologically open to outside help when toxic circumstances seem at the time to be beyond their control (Golan 1978; Brockopp 1973). This is certainly the case with respect to child sexual abuse (Furniss 1991). Unfortunately, in many of these situations, the prolonged investigative period can result in a protracted state of institutional trauma in which families recoil from the tension and confusion they associate with outside professionals disrupting the stability and security of the family. Many families totally close themselves to the outside world, becoming 'emotional fortresses.' This circumstance makes it particularly hard for mental health practitioners to reach these families, to provide the long-term treatment required in situations of child sexual abuse.

Furniss (1983) differentiates between three basic types of intervention that face families contending with such a disclosure. First, there is a 'primary police intervention' that focuses on perpetrator disposition and aims to collect evidence, facilitate the determination of guilt and dispense punishment when crime has been proven. Next, there is a 'primary social service intervention' that has the child as its focus and seeks to protect the physical, emotional and moral well-being of children on behalf of the state. Finally, there is the 'primary therapeutic intervention' that involves an effort to ameliorate the toxic effects of child sexual abuse on all family members, and to assist each person towards more positive mental health and social functioning. Herbert, Grams, and Trute (1986) describe the typical service process in situations of child sexual abuse as a 'linear' one consisting of three stages: abuse assessment, protective intervention, and therapy. Different professional domains (e.g., police, probation, child protection, and mental health) are often involved at each stage. Conflict over the course and focus of intervention can arise any time as service providers (who represent a divergent cross-section of professional backgrounds) set different service priorities in their response to child sexual abuse.

What can be done to improve this unfortunate situation, where incompatible service priorities and objectives seem to prevail in community services responding to child sexual abuse? Both practice experience and research findings provide a strong argument that collaboration among involved agencies increases both the effectiveness of the intervention and the overall quality of services (Finkelhor et al. 1982; Furniss 1991). MacFarlane and Bulkley (1982), conducting a study to determine which factors led to successful collaborations, found that they tended to result from the initiative of individual workers rather than solely through formal policy changes at senior organizational levels.

Effective service coordination at the field level seems critical. There seems to be a need to maintain a service response in which one individual or agency assumes formal responsibility for the coordination of each sexual abuse case, from disclosure through to the termination of early treatment processes. This individual person or agency would function as a connector and interpreter between all parties involved. This would include coordinating and facilitating activities among police, criminal justice departments, health care agencies, and child welfare systems. It would also include facilitation of communication between those investigating the abuse, those providing treatment, and members of the family in which incest has occurred.

The use of a service coordinator has been found to facilitate more effective child abuse services in rural and urban areas. Sefcik and Ormsby (1978) highlighted the functions of such a position, as it was created in south-central Indiana, to essentially include (1) the ongoing clarification of agency roles and relationships in dealing with child abuse and (2) the prevention of service overlap while ensuring delivery of essential services. Helfer and Schmidt (1976) proposed a coordinated approach in responding to child abuse and neglect in urban and rural settings in the United States. They call for more centralized control of child abuse services at the state level rather than the county level in American communities, and suggest the·creation of unified programs that would serve a catchment area with a population base of approximately half a million people. Each of these unified programs would have three basic components: (1) acute care and diagnostic assessment, (2) long-term therapy, and (3) education, training, and research. They envisioned each component as requiring unique (although not entirely separate) coordination functions. A key figure in this plan is the program coordinator, who acts as a facilitator to enhance case diagnosis and long-term abuse treatment as well as professional and community education regarding the prevention and treatment of child abuse and neglect. The formal creation of a service coordinator position specifically for child sexual abuse services was the major thrust of the Pacific Coast Model, which Herbert, Grams, and Trute (1986) proposed to serve communities in the Province of British Columbia in Canada.

The Manitoba Rural Child Sexual Abuse Project

The intent of the Manitoba Rural Child Sexual Abuse Project was to implement a coordinated service model in a rural region under the sponsorship of a local child welfare agency within the Province of Manitoba in Canada. The demonstration project was to involve the design, implementation, and evaluation of a coordinated service approach spanning the investigation and early treatment of intrafamilial child sexual abuse. This three-year project, which serves as the basis for this book, involved the participation of two rural Manitoba locales: south-central Manitoba as the 'test site,' and south-eastern Manitoba as the 'comparison site.' Close similarities were confirmed between these two geographic areas in terms of familial, ethnic, cultural, and economic characteristics. Further, when analyses of families that entered the project in test and comparison areas were completed, the emerging cases were found to be closely similar, in both children and parents, with respect to the psychological response to the assault, the level of overall family functioning and the nature of social-network resources available to families. Both areas were also found to have similar frequencies of child sexual abuse that involved similar types of assault by similar types of perpetrators. Overall it was established that the project involved two highly matched cohorts of cases from two highly matched community settings. (Chapter 6 offers detailed comparisons of the two research communities involved in the Manitoba Rural Child Sexual Abuse Project. It also describes the clients served in both geographic locales.)

Key Components of the Rural Manitoba Approach to Coordinated Services

In essence the project involved the creation of three special service-delivery roles essential to our approach to coordinated services. First, the position of **Service Coordinator** served a pivotal function in the integrated service system. Responsibilities of the service coordinator included acting as an overseer to ensure that all participating service agencies were proceeding in a planned and integrated manner following each disclosure of child sexual abuse. This person also functioned as a connector and interpreter between all parties involved, coordinating activities among police, child protection workers, members of the criminal justice system, members of the medical system, and mental health treatment providers. Immediately following a disclosure, the service coordinator in turn facilitated the involvement of a **Parent Support Worker**. This person provided short-term crisis-intervention services to 'non-offending' parents, which involved planning for the safety of the children in the family, mobilizing the parents as positive resources to the victims, and assisting parents to plan for the next steps in the life of the family. The service coordinator also tracked cases through the investigative phase and made sure a **Case Manager** was assigned for each child and family member who required treatment. The case manager, in consultation with the investigative child welfare worker, parent support worker, and service coordinator, was responsible for preparing a treatment plan, identifying treatment providers, and monitoring the delivery of a sequential, systematic treatment plan.

Several key community planning and coordination activities were essential to the implementation and maintenance of this coordinated service strategy. The first step involved managerial staff from all participating community agencies in a series of meetings aimed at developing commitment and building ongoing administrative support for the coordinated approach. The next stage involved contacting all 'line workers' who might be potential participants (e.g., child welfare workers, police, crown attorneys, physicians, probation service staff, community mental health practitioners) in order to solidify their personal commitment. Following this, a major step was the building and strengthening of a community action group. This group evolved into a **Community Treatment Committee** that met regularly to address interagency service-delivery issues, to provide opportunities for case consultation, and to serve as a vehicle for ongoing professional education in the treatment of child sexual abuse.

Part 1 of this book (Chapters 2 to 5) contains a detailed consideration of the key elements involved in the creation and maintenance of a rural coordinated service system. Chapter 2 focuses on the special context of services that operate in rural communities. The basic steps in building the community infrastructure for interagency consultation and collaboration are offered in Chapter 3 followed, in Chapter 4, by the important linkage between investigative and treatment services, and detailed case histories that track critical service elements. The special need for early response or crisis intervention services is considered, and practical directives for these time-limited and parent-strengthening efforts are highlighted, in Chapter 5.

The Impact of Coordinated Investigation and Treatment Services

Empirical indicators of service impact were collected throughout the term of the demonstration project. Readers who wish to study the evaluation component of the project, and consider related statistical findings, may refer to the final project report, 'Design and Implementation of a Coordinated Community Response to Intra-familial Child Sexual Abuse: The Manitoba Rural Child Sexual Abuse Project' (Adkins, Trute, MacDonald, McCannell, Herbert, Hill, & Scuse

1991). We have attempted, when presenting the empirical findings of our demonstration project, to trim down research jargon and statistical details that may be foreign to practitioners and policy makers. Our intent is to highlight the salient research findings with a minimum use of statistical terminology and to further explicate statistical findings through the use of service examples and client vignettes.[1] This presentation strategy was purposefully employed to provide information in a format that would facilitate its wider dissemination to those who would most likely use the information in community settings; that is, line-level service practitioners, program administrators, and those in senior government positions with responsibility for policy development relating to child abuse services.

Part 2 (Chapters 6, 7, and 8) reviews key research findings encompassing a wide scope of service evaluation, including the use of service-impact indicators at three levels: clients, service agencies, and communities. These chapters consider salient study findings that can assist in the planning and delivery of integrated and effective community services that respond to child sexual abuse.

Chapter 6 offers an overview of the overall evaluation strategy employed within the Manitoba Rural Child Sexual Abuse Project, including a detailed description of the two communities and agencies that participated in the demonstration project. As described in Chapter 7, an important feature of the demonstration project was that the bulk of the staff involved in community treatment services were regular employees of human service agencies in the local rural area. The project did not involve urban-based professionals with extensive expertise in child sexual abuse who would act as temporary consultants to the existing service providers, offering advice as to service direction, then leaving service providers on their own. The objective was to facilitate local community involvement in the design and implementation of a coordinated service plan and to strengthen local service providers in all aspects of child sexual abuse service delivery. Special consideration was given to tracking service delivery patterns, with focused attention given to child and family service workers, because they formed the central core of our model of coor-

---

[1] All names and identifying information are modified in these case vignettes to protect confidentiality. Some case examples contain composite information from several different but actual family situations.

dinated rural services. Chapter 7 also considers the implications of this model, particularly with respect to staffing levels and worker deployment.

Chapter eight briefly describes the service outcome measures that were collected over the term of the project. First, it is argued that the initial crisis resources offered by the Parent Support Services were of important benefit to parents coping with a disclosure of sexual abuse in both test locales (those receiving coordinated services) and comparison locales (those receiving 'normal' interagency services). These services were found to be associated with more positive parent adjustment to the crisis of disclosure and reduced psychological distress in non-offending parents. When service-outcome assessments were completed at the termination of the service-tracking phase of the project, it appeared that parents in the test locale continued to show – and maintain – improved psychological functioning. However, those in the comparison area did not show a corresponding improvement but remained at a higher level of psychological distress.

Overall findings supported the contention that coordinated services do result in more rapid and maintained psychological functioning in those holding major parenting duties; that is, those central to the family's ability to cope following a disclosure of child sexual abuse. According to post-treatment follow-up interviews, service recipients in the coordinated treatment area reported higher levels of satisfaction in their contacts with child welfare personnel. As well, it was found that clients in the coordinated service area had access to substantially higher levels of treatment resources, such as group treatment for children, individual counselling for perpetrators, and group treatment for juvenile perpetrators. A positive spinoff of the coordinated-service approach appeared to be a heightened mobilization of local treatment resources.

To indicate the impact of the coordinated service approach at the community level, Part 3 of this book considers the professional attitudes towards child sexual abuse held by police, child welfare workers, and community mental health workers surveyed throughout the term of the project. At the onset, findings corroborated prior research indicating that such differences did indeed exist. The most notable differences (after analyses were considered for the gender factor) involved the divergence in view concerning priorities in service delivery: police highlighted the need for 'punishment as a deterrent'; other human service professionals emphasized the need for 'treatment to end abuse.' These attitudes remained unchanged throughout the term of the project, a finding highlighting the presence of important ideological differences between key actors in the investigation and treatment of child sexual abuse.

Maintaining collaborative efforts that transcend ideological differences between human service professionals, and in particular between police and child welfare personnel, was seen as a challenging requirement of any coordinated community system for the investigation and early treatment of child sexual abuse. Interagency differences in professional attitude are also considered in Chapter 9, followed by our conclusions and recommendations in Chapter 10.

2

Service Delivery in Rural Communities

The special context of human service practice in the rural community is well recognized in the human service literature, and thoughtful commentaries on the subject are available for both mental health services (Berry & Davis 1978) and family therapy services (Bagarozzi 1982). However, while rural areas share many unique features when compared to urban locales, it is important to acknowledge that there is tremendous diversity across rural communities. Rural areas can vary widely in terms of their population size and density, agricultural base and economic infra-structure, religious and cultural homogeneity, level of crime and social disintegration, or political conservatism. This means that general statements regarding rural life or human services in rural settings must be qualified when considering any particular community or geographic locale. With this understanding in mind, we wish to consider the attributes of rural community settings that can come into play when one considers the coordination of investigative and treatment services in response to child sexual abuse.

The Issue of Travel Distances and Costs

Because of the more dispersed population patterns found in rural locales, those in need of services and those delivering services must often contend with costs associated with frequent and distant travel. This can create serious access issues. For service recipients it means that assistance is difficult to obtain without a willingness to devote the time, money, and energy required to travel to a nearby town or city. For most service providers it means that a significant proportion of an agency's budget must be dedicated to staff transportation costs related to investigative efforts and treatment services. Further, when there is a serious attempt to coordinate community services – child welfare agencies, police, mental health and probation departments, and other allied services that respond to problems of family violence – special financial resources are required simply to bring all the professionals together to one central location so that they can meet on a regular basis. Although telephone communication can greatly facilitate collaborative communication, there is a need for face-to-face meetings to exchange sensitive information, resolve differences of opinion or service disputes, and provide an opportunity for shared, creative case planning.

Community Visibility and Social Stigma

Because of low population density, which is a characteristic of most rural communities, there is a heightened awareness of neighbours' identities and activities and often less social privacy. This can be beneficial, in that it can lead to heightened mutual support and the early identification of serious social or health problems (Huessy 1969). Workers in a small community may have the added advantage of seeing a client function within many spheres of social activity (e.g., coffee shop, church, curling rink, etc.). Coordination between various human service agencies is easier because there are a more limited number of service providers working in a larger catchment area. This facilitates interprofessional access and the sharing of service information, the monitoring of follow-up activities, and the completion of service referrals.

However, the higher visibility that a rural community provides can also raise concerns about social stigma and the violation of personal privacy. Because child sexual abuse is a serious violation of social norms, one that is characterized by shame and powerful social sanctions, the process of denial can pervade families, professional service networks, and the community as a whole. Professionals can feel under subtle but strong community pressure not to move quickly on a disclosure of sexual abuse, but to ensure that adequate proof has been secured before any formal 'labelling' is done or any identifications made. Making the distinction between whether an

act by a parent involves 'sexualized touching,' or 'affectionate caressing', can be difficult to do at the best of times. It is particularly
difficult when the social stakes are dangerously high both in the
family system and in the surrounding community.

One of the prevailing beliefs among those providing mental health
services is that there is a great tolerance for social deviancy in rural
communities, and that a social label that carries a serious stigma
(such as 'mentally ill' or 'child abuser') is applied to one's relative
or neighbour only if it is blatantly obvious (Tranel 1970). However,
it is believed that once this label is formally applied by a human-
service professional (or any other authority with status) in the community, it is extremely difficult for the person thus labelled to immediately contest it or eventually lose it. This situation may be grad-
ually changing as rural populations become more informed about
mental health and social issues (such as family violence and sexism)
because of increases in basic educational levels, efforts by the mass
media, influence of the mental health movement, and the decen-
tralization of public mental health services (Berry & Davis 1978;
Edgerton & Bentz 1969).

Lack of Social Anonymity in Rural Professionals

Child welfare workers, police, and community mental health personnel in most urban agencies can do their jobs and, at the same
time, manage to maintain a separate and private personal life. In
rural locales, however, the separation of work life and personal life
can be difficult to maintain. Professional life in farming communities
and small town settings can easily overlap with one's social life,
participation in community activities, or local shopping ventures.
Because fewer people are participating in community activities, clear
professional boundaries are more difficult to define and maintain.
Once a professional is known to be involved in an investigation
of child abuse, he or she will not easily be trusted in a treatment
role on behalf of a family. For example, if a professional is privy
to highly personal information regarding sexuality within the family,
normal sharing of social roles with members of the family in church
or recreational activities can be compromised. Being identified as
someone who is mandated to investigate crime and uphold the law
(such as a child protection worker or a police officer) can also bring
social isolation from neighbours in a close-knit rural community.

Often these professionals (particularly members of the Royal Canadian Mounted Police) do not remain for extended periods of time in any one community, but are transferred to other locales, further limiting the development of social roots or long-term social relationships. A professional role can thus mean a lonely existence.

Many human service workers in rural settings can also find themselves isolated from other professionals for long periods of time, particularly if they are based in a small village rather than a central town or city. There can be protracted periods in which there is little professional stimulation, access to meaningful practice supervision, or availability of continuing education. This situation is particularly stressful for rural professionals, such as physicians and child abuse investigators, who are usually overworked and have too large caseloads and too long over-extended hours.

In summary, the social loneliness, paucity of important professional resources, and unrelenting work stress in rural settings can heighten the risk of professional burnout.

Guarding Client Confidentiality

Some rural residents liken their community life to 'living in a fishbowl'; that is, their movements around the community and participation in its social life are open to easy observation. Confidentiality of private personal matters is seen to need special protection. Often human service professionals such as mental health practitioners will be extremely careful to ensure that a confidence is not divulged. If they are identified in the rural community as people who will let private matters become known to others, they will quickly lose their credibility and their clients. Lack of discretion can also hinder what would be appropriate service alternatives in the urban setting, such as group therapy or multi-family interventions. Such clinical interventions can be compromised when they involve people that closely share other social or community ties.

To professionals who are sensitive to such elements of 'small-town culture,' doubts can arise about whether they should release sensitive client information to other professionals (even to an agency that has referred a client directly to them). This can result in interagency distrust and hostility. It can also lead to the hoarding of clients or a hesitancy to make necessary referrals to other appropriate agencies, which seems often to be wrapped in the noble mantle of 'information confidentiality.' Thus, professionals can feel trapped in a service double bind: they either risk leaks in confidentiality, which will cause clients to stay away; or they risk withholding service information, which can alienate allied agencies and weaken collaborative, comprehensive services for their clients.

A Special Kind of Isolation: Ideological Loneliness

When he reviewed a past decade of his experience as a psychiatrist with a rural practice, Gurian (1971) reflected that 'Rural areas more than urban areas are inclined to be politically conservative, so a certain type of cultural alienation goes along with the professional loneliness' (p. 57). When one considers this cultural alienation with respect to child sexual abuse, it can be seen as a circumstance in which the professionals can be quite ideologically estranged from their surrounding community. It is not uncommon for professionals to find themselves wrestling with the widespread belief that child sexual abuse is a rare phenomenon that involves what is often considered deranged or allegedly deviant (e.g., mentally deficient or homosexual) perpetrators. It is not uncommon for professionals dealing with allegations of child sexual abuse to find minimization and misinformation operating in such important sectors of the rural community as churches or service clubs. While these practitioners can more easily find and associate with 'kindred spirits' in urban settings, those who work directly with child sexual abuse in rural communities often report a 'wall of denial' that pervades community life and that can erode one's energy and convictions.

Most professionals working in child abuse services recognize that inherent in the widespread family violence that pervades our society is an adherence to 'patriarchal belief systems' that perpetuate attacks on the person and bodies of women and children (Herman 1981; Herman & Hirschman 1977). In rural communities that tend towards political and religious conservatism, there is a heightened presence of such patriarchal attitudes and authoritarianism, particularly as these relate to male domination and sexist values (Bagarozzi 1982), and to family roles and responsibilities (Berry & Davis 1978). When one works in the child sexual abuse field, it is essential that there is a heightened awareness of one's own values and beliefs about patriarchy, gender roles, sexuality, and violence. These can create additional work-related stressors for rural practitioners who are attempting to reduce and treat child sexual abuse, particularly those who feel surrounded by a destructive and distorted community ideology and who feel alone in their struggle to cope with it.

Concentration of Authority

In rural settings, basic human-service sectors (e.g., child welfare, community mental health, the courts) do not employ large numbers of people. They are also usually managed locally by a few individuals in key positions who can hold strategic importance for setting service priorities and policies. This situation can be beneficial: it can create opportunities for unencumbered decision-making and facilitate easier collaboration between the few actors holding program authority. However, it also makes some communities prisoners of the idiosyncracies of individual leadership and vulnerable to inflexible decision-making. For example, if the area has only one judge who presides in criminal court, and that person opposes changes in regular court procedures (such as alternative sentencing), it can bog down attempts to integrate family treatment with perpetrator sentencing in cases such as those involving father-daughter incest. Or, if a director of the local mental health service takes a conservative and narrow stance on what services should be delivered by his or her staff (e.g., holds the line on the operating budget), or if he or she only allows travel in the rural area for the provision of direct or face-to-face service to clients, this will effectively block any attempts to have community mental health workers participate in interagency professional meetings (which usually do not involve any direct contact with a client). This in turn can disable attempts to involve a community mental health program in a coordinated service system. Depending on the intransigence of such people in authority and the scope of their influence in the community-service response to child sexual abuse, their impact on coordinated services can vary greatly. It can be either a blessing or a curse to have decision-making consolidated in the hands of so few key authorities.

Recruitment of Human Service Personnel

The bulk of professional training programs are located in urban centres. It is difficult to attract highly trained people to rural areas. This is particularly true of experts in the treatment of family violence. People trained in urban settings tend to want to continue practising in urban settings. Many highly trained human service professionals who practise in rural locales do not stay there long but tend to be attracted back to the urban workplace after a stint of rural living. Many who have remained for the long term in rural settings do over time amass extensive and comprehensive practice experience. However, proportionally few of them, as compared to their urban colleagues, will have the advanced training that child sexual abuse services require. There is thus a tendency for rural agencies to attempt to refer challenging cases, such as those involving incest, to the specialized treatment centres, usually located in nearby cities.

The development of local child sexual abuse treatment resources is thus not a trivial matter in most rural areas. It requires the participation of highly motivated practitioners who are willing to stretch their already burdened professional lives, the creation of extensive in-service training opportunities relating to the treatment of family violence (for both front-line and supervisory staff), and the commitment of scarce program funding from the key participating human service agencies. It takes formal recognition by responsible program administrators that child sexual abuse is a serious issue in rural areas. Further, it takes professional courage in the local human service personnel *themselves* if they are to do something substantial to deal directly with it.

Generalist Practitioners within Specialized Service Sectors

Berry and Davis (1978) acknowledge that the rural practitioner must be a generalist capable of providing a variety of interventions, because the rural community cannot afford many specialists or different referral sites. It is difficult therefore to mobilize treatment resources in which boundaries of professional identity and role are carefully maintained. In urban settings it may be possible (and perhaps advisable) to have child protection workers doing only protection work and not extending themselves into family counselling, or to have family mental health treatment delivered solely by mental health specialists (Thorman 1983). In rural settings, because professional expertise is at a premium, more flexibility in treatment roles is required if local treatment programs are to be developed. This can create stress in service providers who feel their time, energy, and therapeutic skills are stretched to the limit. On the other hand, those professionals who tend to be bored with narrow service responsibilities may find such generalist treatment services stimulating and energizing, as well as an opportunity to expand their therapeutic abilities and widen their professional contribution in their home community.

In this chapter we have attempted to highlight the most salient implications of delivering coordinated child sexual abuse services in rural settings. It is evident that the rural context will create both advantages and disadvantages in the provision of these services. Certainly, these rural factors must be carefully considered and directly addressed when planning and implementing coordinated rural services that respond to child sexual abuse.

3

Community Coordination of Child Sexual Abuse Services

The reported incidence of child sexual abuse has increased dramatically throughout Canada and North America, while investigation and treatment services have tended to be uncoordinated and sporadic (Badgley Report 1984; Finkelhor, Gomes-Schwartz, & Horowitz 1982; MacFarlane & Bulkley, 1982). In responding to child sexual abuse, rural areas are particularly vulnerable to shortages of service resources. At the present time most professionals working in the area of child sexual abuse advocate a coordinated, multidisciplinary approach. Sgroi (1982) identifies the essential steps that need to be taken in implementing such an approach. These include (1) the creation of a group of competent specialists in child sexual abuse, (2) the assignment of more than one professional to work with a family in which incest occurs, (3) the regular and formal review of all cases involving child sexual abuse, and (4) the creation of a variety of treatment alternatives. Because sexual abuse issues involve many different services (e.g., medical, legal, child welfare, and mental health), there is a need for practitioners in the different participating service areas to understand each other's perspectives and collaborate closely with each other if they are to create effective intervention plans for the children and their families. While few dispute this hypothesis, research findings regarding the outcome of such multidisciplinary responses have been mixed.

Tucker (1979) reviewed the literature on interagency coordination and concluded, 'We do not know whether consciously planned and implemented patterns of coordination amongst service providers facilitates the solving of social and individual problems.' Benjamin (1981) evaluated the use of multidisciplinary teams in providing services to child abusing families and concluded that such teams were generally inefficient and ineffective. More recent research continues to be inconclusive. A study conducted at McMaster University (Byles 1985), which examined the hypothesis that interagency collaboration would provide more efficient and effective services to abused children and their families, never reached the testing stage because of complex problems during the process of project development. These centred around the issue of interagency power struggles, conflict between research objectives and service priorities, and struggles with respect to case management and information confidentiality. Byles concluded that there is a need for more studies of interagency programs in order to identify elements that foster either success or failure.

In contrast, Hochstadt and Harwicke (1985) assessed the effectiveness of a multidisciplinary approach in the Chicago area and concluded that the approach was effective. This analysis included the review of the number of recommended services obtained by a sample of 180 children one year after a multidisciplinary evaluation was implemented, as compared to a previous sample of children who had not received such treatment. The 'multidisciplinary team' in this instance was a newly formed, specialized team housed in a single children's hospital agency; it did not include a wide range of human service agencies in shared case management. MacFarlane and Bulkley (1982) also conducted a study to determine which factors led to successful collaborations and found that they tended to result from individual workers taking the initiative, rather than formal policy changes at senior levels within government departments.

The Manitoba Rural Child Sexual Abuse Project was designed to investigate the effectiveness of a coordinated, multiagency treatment approach to the complex problem of child sexual abuse within rural community settings. In planning this model, it was recognized that direct collaboration at the field level was critical: that is, it was taken as a given that local service providers would need to take an active role in the design and implementation of any coordinated service system. In its broadest sense the goal of the project was to create an integrated model of service delivery in the area of child sexual abuse, by bringing together a diverse group of human service agencies in a rural area and assisting them to develop a shared sense of purpose and direction in the handling of these cases.

Five components were identified as essential to the creation of the community service infrastructure necessary for a coordinated community approach. In the sequence in which they were developed in the project, the components were

1.   the establishment of a service coordinator position in the geographic locale containing the service network;

2.   the garnering of commitment from senior managerial levels of all key participating agencies;

3.   the holding of initial planning meetings with all parties involved in the investigation and treatment of child sexual abuse (i.e., child welfare protection and treatment workers, police, crown attorneys, judges, probation workers, and physicians);

4.   the establishment of regular meetings of investigative, legal, and treatment personnel;

5.   the establishment of a parent support worker (PSW) position to provide immediate crisis counselling services to non-offending parents at the time of the disclosure of child sexual abuse.

Once an infrastructure for coordinated community service was in place, integrated investigative and treatment services proceeded through three sequential stages: Stage One: Coordinated investigative action by police and the child welfare department; Stage Two: legal-investigatory decision-making regarding treatment; Stage Three: systemic treatment of intrafamilial child sexual abuse. These stages involved the coordination of services through key steps that spanned investigation and early treatment services, including interlinked police and child welfare investigations. This was immediately followed by the development and implementation of a coordinated intervention plan for each specific case. A family-centred systems perspective (Hartman & Laird 1983) framed the design of each treatment plan which was consistent with Trepper and Barrett's multiple systems model (1986).

Key Steps in the Design of the Coordinated System

Each of the major steps in the initial design of the coordinated service system is described here. In addition, factors that appeared to hinder or facilitate each step are considered.

Establishment of a Service Coordinator Position

The service coordinator position was vital to the integrated service system. The service coordinator's primary duties included (a) *taking a leadership position in promoting coordination between the various service agencies and professional disciplines responding to child sexual abuse.* The service coordinator was to establish an orderly transition between the investigative stage and the treatment stage of services by meeting with the child and family services[1] (CFS) investigative worker, the parent support worker, and the assigned case manager to discuss the progress of each referred family and to plan treatment goals; (b) *establishing open and regular interagency communication* with police, physicians, crown attorneys, and the CFS agency lawyer (In coordinating the treatment aspect of child sexual abuse, the service coordinator was to hold regular meetings with each case manager to review case progress and to discuss ongoing service coordination efforts.); (c) *establishing and maintaining ongoing, regular meetings of the local community treatment team* (The purpose and goals of these meetings will be discussed later in this chapter.); (d) *developing and promoting interagency training opportunities* involving Community Mental Health and Mental Retardation Services, Child and Family Services, and other key participating agencies; (e) *promoting public awareness* in local communities with respect to child sexual abuse; and (f) *providing education for key 'gatekeepers'* involved in disclosure and identification of child abuse (e.g., teachers, clergy, daycare workers).

Garnering Commitment from Senior Managerial Levels in Key Participating Agencies

From the onset, the importance of obtaining support for the coordinated approach from the management of each human-service

---

[1] In the Province of Manitoba, child welfare agencies are referred to as child and family services. The terms child and family services (or CFS) and child welfare agency are both used in this book.

agency involved in situations of child sexual abuse was recognized. Thus, a preliminary step in system development was to meet with supervisors of each participating agency on an individual basis to enlist their cooperation. During these meetings the goals of the coordinated approach and the potential levels of participation required from each service sector were outlined. These meetings were seen as essential in building management-level support for a functional, collaborative working relationship between field-level professionals. The importance of addressing any interagency issues of concern (such as past service tensions or disputes) was highlighted at this stage in the planning of the coordinated service system.

One of the major questions raised by the local service providers was how each agency was going to benefit from this approach to service delivery. Training and consultation opportunities were emphasized as key potential benefits that would be available to all participants. The importance of coordination to facilitate better service delivery, thereby providing better service for the clients of every agency, was emphasized as an important community benefit. It was also hoped that coordination of services and increased collaboration between agencies would ultimately reduce the overall service demands of child sexual abuse cases for individual service providers.

A key concern at this early stage was the over-extension of existing resources already being experienced by community agencies. Supervisors from several local agencies commented that it was frightening to commit to something new when they were already taxed to the limit. It was acknowledged that coordination, if effective, should lessen feelings of overload because of the extra collegial support provided. It was recognized that most agencies were dealing individually with sexual abuse cases already, even though this may not have been seen specifically as their primary service mandate. The coordination would hopefully provide a more effective vehicle for service delivery and thereby relieve some of the burden created by service fragmentation. Consider the following case study:

It was difficult to involve Community Mental Health Services (CMH) at the onset of the project as a participating member. There were a number of reasons for the difficulty with this agency. First, CMH may have anticipated a more major role in the project (perhaps that of a formal sponsoring agency in the research grant submission), and may have felt invalidated by the course of action that had been taken.

Second, CMH did not specifically see the problem of child sexual abuse as falling directly within its purview. It seemed that CMH caseloads in the research locale tended to be more heavily weighted with clients with chronic mental health problems; that is, those clients that would clearly fall under the aegis of the Manitoba Mental Health Act and who could be readily identified within the terms of the DSM-III. Indeed, one CMH worker noted that since child sexual abuse was not in the DSM-III, he felt he should not have to deal with it.

In initial discussions preceding the onset of the project, CMH had been considered an agency that might provide a seconded position to the project. When this did not materialize, some resentment was experienced. There was a sense of 'CFS got it all, why were we left out?' In addressing these concerns, it was important to acknowledge the importance of CMH's role and to focus on the learning, with respect to the treatment of child sexual abuse, that mental health workers might access through participation in the project. In the end, the mental health coordinator deferred to the wishes of his line workers concerning the degree of their participation in the project. Fortunately, the mental health line workers serving in the test community of the research project were quite enthusiastic about participating as treatment providers within the coordinated model.

Concerns were also expressed regarding professional territorial issues (i.e., who has control over the intervention process). The supervisors in each participating agency were reassured that each worker would maintain control over what was done with his or her clients by that worker. The service coordinator would ensure service integration through open interagency communication, and would provide consultation when appropriate regarding a collaborative treatment approach. In cases of disagreement, the service coordinator would meet with treatment providers, the case manager (this position will be described later in this chapter) and, if necessary, the supervisors of the individual treatment providers to discuss the interagency disagreement. In situations of interprofessional dispute as to how a case should proceed, the service coordinator would attempt to reach a mutually satisfactory understanding of how to best proceed with a case. If consensus was not possible, the final service choices would rest with each agency responsible for the ongoing progress of the case. It seems to be an essential tenet of any coordinated approach that agencies will generally refuse to have

service planning taken entirely out of their hands. It is a circumstance that is well deserving of recognition and respect.

In any community, human service agencies have a 'service history.'
When the past has been marked by conflict, this can create a barrier
to any formal agreement regarding close collaboration in service
delivery. One example:

There was some difficulty in gaining initial managerial support for
collaborative efforts involving the Family Violence Program (FVP)
and Child and Family Services (CFS). The relationship with CFS
and FVP had been strained historically. Trust on both sides was
low, largely due to the different philosophies held by each agency
and the lack of understanding of each other's position. FVP focused
on supporting and protecting the privacy of the non-offending parent. They had felt in the past that CFS was insensitive to the needs
and feelings of the non-offending parent and believed that CFS
tended to support the child without recognition of the issues faced
by the mother. However, when these concerns were alleviated
through discussion, FVP was able to support the project and recognize how it could be of value to them. They recognized the training
and consultation opportunities and saw this as a way of gaining an
increased understanding of the other agency's perspectives.

A related interagency problem was that, although *initial* managerial support for coordination was secured, it seemed that *ongoing*
support was not easily maintained at a sufficiently high level. In
other words, the managers gave their initial verbal support but did
not actively promote and encourage the efforts of their field workers
when they participated on treatment teams. In addition, the managers did not become personally involved in service coordination,
and tended not to see it as an issue they should actively consider.
The implications of this for the successful continuance of the collaborative model will be addressed later.

*Planning Meeting with All Parties Directly Involved in Investigation and
Treatment of Child Sexual Abuse*

After achieving basic managerial support, which included a formal
agreement to participate by each community agency, the second

stage in the process was activated: line workers were asked to attend
a meeting of all community professionals involved in dealing with
child sexual abuse cases. This initial meeting was well attended and
proved to be helpful in initiating longer-term collaboration between
workers. It had a number of purposes: (1) to solidify the personal
commitment of community professionals, (2) to define the concept
of coordination in local terms, (3) to establish specific goals of service coordination, (4) to identify differing service ideologies with regard to case identification and management, (5) to explore each party's level of commitment to coordination through their willingness
to delegate service resources, and (6) to have each participating
human-service professional identify his or her personal areas of interest in the treatment of child sexual abuse (e.g., individual or group
treatment with victims or perpetrators, etc.).

This meeting was seen as successful and crucial to the continuing
planning effort. Workers were frank in discussing their negative
concerns as well as their positive expectations. Different ideologies
with regard to the identification and management of cases became
apparent but did not become barriers to ongoing discussion. Workers began to understand more about the stresses and limitations
under which their colleagues operated. For example, a community
mental health worker expressed her concerns regarding the reporting of a sexual abuse disclosure to Child and Family Services of
Central Manitoba. She felt it might move too quickly and from too
polarized a child-advocacy position. She was reassured, however,
that CFS would work collaboratively with her to ensure the disclosure was dealt with in a therapeutic manner. Many community
practitioners expressed concern and scepticism as well about the
legal system and the willingness of this service sector to consult
with others. A number of action plans to build more collaboration
between the crown prosecutor, Child and Family Services, police
and probation services were formulated.

*Establishment of Regular Meetings of Investigative, Legal, and Treatment
Personnel*

During the development of the coordinated community approach,
a major thrust was to build and strengthen the community action
group that had been established initially. Ideally this action group
was seen as consisting of professionals working in (1) the child welfare investigation, (2) the legal investigation and processing, and (3)

the treatment-service spheres responding to child sexual abuse. Unfortunately, as time went on, representatives from the legal service sector (the law-enforcement department and the probation office) did not continue to attend meetings regularly. In some cases this created a gap in the overall effort to create a closely coordinated service response. The community action group, or Community Treatment Committee as it later was called, did meet regularly and consisted of approximately twenty-four to thirty professionals working in the rural locale. It included representatives of Child and Family Services of Central Manitoba, the Community Mental Health Services, Mental Retardation Services, the Family Violence Program, and the Eden Mental Health Centre. Efforts were made to include representation from the schools and churches. This was difficult to arrange because of the secondary involvement of these institutions in child sexual abuse services and the complex steps required to secure the delegation of their representatives.

The goals of the Community Treatment Committee meetings were formalized as follows: (a) to provide practice training sessions on treatment and research issues; (b) to provide a routine opportunity for case consultation; (c) to promote understanding of the service philosophies of the different participating agencies; (d) to explore and deal with professional issues such as territoriality concerns, differences in treatment approaches, and feelings of exclusion; (e) to provide a formal opportunity to share information and knowledge; (f) to work towards the development of a common service language, mutual support, and interprofessional validation; and (g) to provide emotional support to professionals feeling vulnerable and upset when contending with child sexual abuse cases. The community treatment committee met every other week, its agenda focusing on four areas: practice training, case discussion, training in the administration and interpretation of research instruments, and discussion of community interagency coordination issues.

The review of issues in community coordination was a basic and ongoing activity of the community treatment committee. This will be described later. However committee sessions involving (1) training for clinical practice, (2) training in the use of empirical assessment measures, and (3) the use of case presentations for peer consultation were special and time-limited activities. Each is briefly described here.

Clinical practice training sessions

It is important to note that these sessions were largely facilitated by local 'experts' in the social services, who provided training free of charge or for a small honorarium. This underscores the importance of utilizing the professional-development resources available within geographic reach of rural communities rather than relying solely on 'imported experts.' Ongoing community-based training sessions were thus unique in that they were *inter*agency rather than *intra*-agency. Professional training in rural locales is frequently offered only on an agency-by-agency basis, an approach that seems to promote cohesion within a particular agency but not understanding and collaboration across agencies. Helfer and Schmidt (1976) suggest that intra-agency training in child abuse services 'fosters "inbreeding" and traditionalism – and actually inhibits multidisciplinary services programs' (p. 241). Further, they suggest that in-service training that is provided only within one agency setting creates a false assumption among community practitioners that professionals in the other disciplines have been adequately trained to do their jobs in the child abuse field.

An important component towards building a collaborative community approach to services is to provide shared regional training sessions for all professionals who offer services to a target client group. It will facilitate the development of a common knowledge base and – what is vital to collaborative practice – a more clearly shared treatment ideology.

Training in the use of service tracking and clinical assessment measures

All members of the community treatment committee were trained in the use of service-contact forms, registration and intake forms, and treatment outcome measures. A standardized program-information system was designed and implemented consistent with prior protocols established for the human services (Trute, Tefft, & Scuse 1985). Training sessions involving clinical assessment measures focused on the interpretation of the results of these measures in order to help workers gain a sense of their clinical usefulness and to encourage use of the measures as an integral part of the treatment process. Each practitioner who served as a case manager was provided with a manual on how to use, score and interpret each service record and treatment outcome measure. A research assistant was available to meet individually with workers to review the scoring of the project measures and to discuss implications for treatment. Despite this training, many workers continued to feel they were unable to use the treatment outcome measures effectively. Although the research team initially felt they had scheduled adequate assistance in the use of outcome measures, some workers felt it was not extensive enough to meet their individual needs.

The introduction of a program-information system in human service settings is a complex enterprise that is fraught with methodological and political issues (Trute 1983). Training plans need to be carefully considered when implementing a program-information system, particularly when treatment outcome measures are incorporated into the data-retrieval plan. The important need for continuous and individualized training sessions in such information systems should not be underestimated.

Our intent throughout was to monitor all service activities through the use of standard reporting forms to be completed by all community service staff participating in the coordinated community approach. As well, it was decided that clinicians rather than research assistants should administer treatment outcome measures. Because of the highly sensitive circumstances tied to situations of child sexual abuse, we felt that workers who were known to clients would be the best persons to collect social and psychological measures that tracked client functioning. Because of the many people intruding into the lives of families where incest occurred, it was felt that data collection by a research assistant should be avoided because it meant the addition of one more outsider in the life of the family.

However, use of professionals as data-gathering agents was not without its own inherent difficulties. The workers were already heavily strained for time and were used to collecting only key information that was directly linked to court reporting or to meeting recording requirements for their treatment files. In effect we were moving into an environment where workers were not used to routine information collection according to standardized protocols.

The training of workers to collect research information, however limited in scope, is not a trivial matter. As a general rule, when professional workers are responsible for gathering data relating to the progress of clients and services, attention must be paid to providing ongoing consultation to these workers on a regular and frequent basis. Initial training should involve the use of clinical examples highlighting the service relevance of any empirical treatment measures workers are expected to collect. A key to success in this process seems to be each worker's recognition that the clinical measures can be used to facilitate their own practice with their own clients. Those that can see this link seem to be the ones who adopt data gathering more quickly and efficiently. Those who cannot see how the measures will help their own practice, or their clients' progress, have a more difficult time with data-gathering procedures. Workers who are able to integrate the use of the standardized clinical measures in their ongoing clinical practice seem to be the ones who view the clinical measures as helpful in guiding their treatment activities.

Case consultation

Discussion of specific cases proved to be an important and valuable aspect of the community treatment committee meetings. It helped professionals become aware of the struggles each faced in their particular role with the families in which sexual abuse had occurred. For example, treatment providers gained greater understanding of the stresses and dilemmas faced by protection workers, enabling them to build a sense of pulling together on a case rather than opposing one another. The case consultations were also beneficial in enabling workers to receive the support that is so necessary in order to cope with the many stresses that face those working in this field. As an example:

A mental health practitioner presented a case in which she was the case manager. She was feeling frustrated and helpless because the family was not willingly engaging in treatment. The case was one of sibling incest in which a seventeen-year-old brother had molested his five-year-old sister. The boy was involved in treatment with a CFS social worker and the sister attended group therapy. However, the parents were very angry with the judicial system and refused to accept any treatment for themselves. As the worker explored the salient elements of the case during a meeting of the community treatment committee, it became clear that she was accomplishing a great deal in her role as coordinator of the treatment being provided to the children, and she left the meeting feeling revitalized. The case consultation allowed her to extricate herself from the parents' feelings of helplessness and to better focus on the work to be done to move them forward.

While case consultations did provide positive learning experiences for the workers, many difficulties also arose. One of the major issues that surfaced was differing ideologies between workers relating to the management and treatment of victims and perpetrators of child sexual abuse. When these ideologies were openly addressed and discussed, progress was made in building collaboration and understanding among the workers.

It is important that participants view meetings as productive. Meetings were seen as productive when there was an opportunity to share case information, exchange practical knowledge, and develop familiarity with all professional views and opinions. A concern that was expressed regarding the meetings was the lack of commitment from some service sectors, specifically community corrections services, law enforcement agencies, and representatives from the legal system. Workers generally felt that, without a commitment from these areas, the value of the community meetings was diminished, especially since professionals in these areas hold such a key position in determining the consequences of sexual abuse cases. It was agreed that great attention must be paid to attaining commitment from representatives from all key service sectors, including criminal justice department, to attend such community meetings and participate in collaborative case planning if the coordinated approach was to reach its full potential.

Lack of adequate practice supervision was also found to increase each individual worker's sense of professional isolation. Most workers wanted more supervision than they received in the project, which was over and above the usual supervisory resources available in their home agencies. Regular meetings of the community treatment committee and the presence of a service coordinator were structural solutions that helped address this wish for more supervisory resources. However, within this collaborative peer–review structure, it was felt that there must be a willingness to examine the 'internal process of the team' (Dale, Waters, Davies, Roberts

& Morrison 1986). Dale and his colleagues emphasize the need for 'an open exploration of differences.' They state 'in the wider agency and professional world change will only occur if the rigidity of attitudes are examined. It is the process of rigidity, which creates attitudes of paranoia and distrust within the professional system, which is so reminiscent of the atmosphere within the sexually abusing family itself' (p. 23). Regular committee meetings provide one structural means of addressing these differences in the interagency professional service system. However, it takes time, courage, commitment, and considerable skill to address the process issues that emerge.

Having outlined the steps taken to establish a collaborative community service network, the details of a three stage ecological approach implemented for each case situation will be described.

Stages in the Coordinated Community Service Model

Stage One: Synchronizing Investigative Activities by Police and Child Welfare Services

Active collaboration in case planning, by the various professionals involved in the investigative stage, was considered essential in building a coordinated service response. Major actors involved at this stage included child protection services or CFS workers, police, physicians, the crown attorney, and probation services. Figure 3.1 (p. 39) offers a description of the flow of decisions that are required in investigation and early treatment services.

There are several key steps in building service coordination during this phase of service delivery:

a)   Encouragement of joint interviews between police and CFS investigative workers

This did occur regularly, and many of the workers felt that it resulted in better investigations with less trauma for child and family.

b)   Establishment of regular meetings with police, crown attorney and investigative workers to review cases

While an attempt was made to establish such meetings, maintaining this link was extremely difficult. The meetings did not occur on a regular basis and there was often a lack of coordination among the various people involved at this stage. For example, the police and CFS investigative workers sometimes found that they held fundamentally different views on how to proceed with a case. There was sometimes conflict as well with the crown attorney and police and CFS workers. In one situation the Crown Attorney decided not to press charges even though the CFS worker and police felt there was sufficient evidence to proceed. These differences of view were declared, but the lack of regular meetings to coordinate the investigative process made a mutually satisfactory resolution of differences of viewpoint between legal and child welfare authorities very difficult.

c)   Establishment of regular meetings between the investigative workers and the parent support worker

In examining services available to families when a disclosure of child sexual abuse has been made, it was quickly recognized that there was a gap in terms of providing immediate crisis support for non-offending parents. In an attempt to fill this gap, the parent support services were implemented. The role of the parent support worker was to provide brief crisis intervention and psychological support to the non-offending parent(s). This PSW focused on: (i) helping parents understand procedures followed in the investigative process and their rights within this process, (ii) ensuring that there was a 'safety plan' to protect children from further abuse, (iii) providing education regarding sexual abuse and its effects, (iv) assisting parents to be a positive psychological resource to the victimized child, and (v) providing support to assist the non-offending parent with his or her own feelings of despair and sense of victimization. (The role and functions of the parent support worker are more fully described in Chapter 6.)

Meetings between the parent support worker and those conducting the investigation proved to be extremely helpful in dealing with a family's needs during the investigative stage. As well, this facilitated the eventual planning that needed to be done to ensure treatment services for the families in which treatment was later seen to be necessary.

Figure 3.1
Investigation-treatment decisions

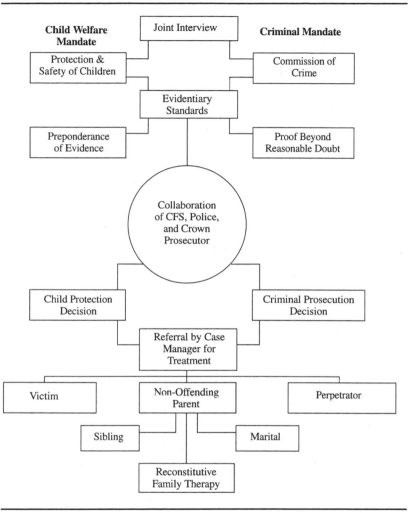

d) Recognition of the importance of encouraging physicians to become involved in both identification and investigation stages.

At the beginning of the project only one physician was primarily consulted in sexual abuse cases. While he was a committed and skilled practitioner, it was felt that enlisting more physicians to work in the area would be helpful. A letter was sent to all physicians in the geographic locale asking if they were interested in working in the area of child sexual abuse and would like to participate in training opportunities. Five physicians responded, and all received training in assault examinations from medical experts. These physicians then continued over the long term to function as medical resources within the local coordinated service system.

Although coordination at this first stage of service delivery was considered essential, many problems arose during our attempts to build more integration between the child welfare department and police investigators:

Coordinating with police

The task of establishing coordination of investigative services with the RCMP proved to be a long and arduous one. There were several reasons for this difficulty. In spite of numerous meetings with various police detachments and a formal directive from the divisional commander, some police investigators did not adhere to Manitoba provincial policy calling for joint consultation on all child abuse allegations. There were a number of reasons for this problem. Some police investigators said they simply did not know the provincial policy – a common problem because new police officers were transferred into rural areas immediately after their initial training, a training that did not adequately prepare them for child sexual abuse investigations. Some claimed they had to conduct such investigations (e.g., in the evening when rapid coordination with CFS was more difficult). Others did not understand that involvement of a child protection agency was required by law, to determine whether the children were safe. In one instance, a police detachment had done its own investigation one week before the referral came to the attention of the child protection agency. The agency had been alerted by a concerned citizen who was providing refuge for a victim refusing to return home. The police had decided, on their own, that because the victim's brother had fondled her on only a 'few' occasions, the case did not warrant serious intervention by anyone.

Contributing to this inability to achieve consistency was the fact that there were seven RCMP detachments and three town police constabularies within the project's geographic area. The sheer number of police investigators made it difficult to reach each one in order to build commitment to coordinated investigative procedures. As well, the RCMP maintain an operating principle of frequent officer transfers, which leads to high staff turnover from detachment to detachment. As a result, an officer who had been adequately introduced to our collaborative investigative procedures would often be moved out of the area. While it was understood that the provincial policy regarding investigative procedures was less of a problem for the RCMP, local town police forces had less training and even less supervision from their governing body, the Manitoba Police Commission. From the investigative procedures initiated in the local area, a number of problems surfaced regularly: the police sometimes used a confrontational style of questioning that was seen by other community practitioners as increasing the possibility that the victim would recant on a disclosure. Even in some highly-charged situations involving frightened children, some police officers believed they should do their investigation in full uniform. This intimidated more vulnerable victims, leaving them feeling they were the ones who had done something wrong.

The intrusion of gender bias

Another aspect to the issue of commitment was gender bias, an issue we believe may have played a part in the hesitancy of the police to collaborate and the department of the Attorney-General to assume more commitment to the concept of coordination of investigations. In the local geographic area, there were no women occupying managerial positions within the police forces, no female police officers doing police investigations, and no women acting as prosecuting attorneys. This predominance of men in the legal – investigatory field suggested a possible predominant male perspective that shaped policy development in the investigation of child sexual abuse, a perspective that seems to be anchored in a patriarchal view of the family. As Rogers (1990) suggested in his summary report on child sexual abuse to the minister of Health and Welfare, 'Our patriarchal society has set the conditions for sexual assaults, and harassment, including the sexual abuse of children' (p. 9). In some instances this patriarchal view was experienced during police questioning, which included enquiries such as, 'Did you do anything to encourage your brother?' 'Do you like dressing up?' 'Did you enjoy it?' Interactions with a number of police investigators led an experienced female social-work investigator to declare that men should not be investigators with responsibility for collecting evidence from sexually abused children. She argued that men tended to minimize the significance of the assaults and could not adequately appreciate a child's feelings of victimization. The use of male investigators in child sexual abuse cases has also been challenged by Frosh (1988), who suggests that men should not do investigative work in this area unless victims know and trust them or are known to trust men more than women.

Commitment of senior authorities

A third factor that had a deleterious effect on establishing coordination meetings with the statutory agencies was the lack of firm direction from senior authorities in the justice system. It seemed that little priority was given to facilitating a coordinated collection of evidence in child sexual abuse cases. While crown attorneys expressed a sincere desire to be present at coordinating meetings, they often were unable to attend because of pressing time constraints. The issue of time management was in fact an important element in defeating a more coordinated approach for all the statutory agencies. At the beginning of the project, a tentative agreement was reached between the Crown, the police, and the child protection agency. They agreed to discuss the disposition of each upcoming case in the criminal court building immediately after a court session, as this was the only time the Crown could make available.

While this was attempted in a number of cases, the logistics of such meetings proved unworkable. Child welfare investigators were pressured by the rising numbers of new cases; police conducted investigations during their shift of duty. This combination of time constraints across professional groups from different service sectors made it extremely difficult to arrange coordinated planning of investigative activities on a case-by-case basis. Because there were so many different police investigators, located in many different geographical locales and working under the auspices of differing governing bodies, it proved difficult to maintain child sexual abuse cases as a priority down through the chain of command. Even while the inspector and staff sergeant in the project area were strongly committed, their commitment did not translate to a line level of approximately seventy investigators. Again, the varied statutes requiring police investigation made it difficult for police to focus much attention on child sexual abuse.

Standards of evidence

Finally, commitments from the justice agencies to the concept of coordination were affected by issues of ideology and legal interpretation. This was most obvious in the different spheres of criminal law and family law. From these two courts, statutory decisions involving child sexual abuse cases are made from two different perspectives, with different purposes, requiring two separate standards of proof. From the criminal court perspective, investigations are done to determine if a crime has been committed and to determine fair punishment. In the criminal court, the standard of proof is 'proof beyond a reasonable doubt.' In contrast, child-welfare investigations, under the aegis of the family court, are carried out to ensure the protection and safety of children using as the standard of proof a 'preponderance of evidence' and the 'balance of probabilities.' These differing purposes and standards of proof sometimes interfered with the ability of the investigating agencies (i.e., police and child welfare) to come to an agreement about how a case should proceed with regard to the gathering and preparation of evidence that might lead to charges being laid.

In this respect, police investigators and crown prosecutors most often looked for clear medical or physical evidence that a child had been molested, even though child sexual assaults often do not leave any clear evidence of this kind. In fact, most often such assaults are committed in the absence of witnesses and involve bribery or threats, and many cases of child sexual abuse leave no physical evidence. This reliance on medical and physical evidence, according to Heger and Summit (1981), is complexly related to our society's and community's need not to know or to ignore that the sexual abuse of children is a widespread problem.

In one example, a case of father – son incest, a struggle occurred between the child protection agency and the investigating police regarding the laying of criminal charges. It was a case that highlighted many of the problems in developing a coordinated service in response to child sexual abuse:

Mr and Mrs K and their five children lived in a small rural community some distance from a local RCMP detachment. They had immigrated to Canada in recent years. One evening Mrs. K informed the police that she believed her husband 'had sex' with the family dog. The police apprehended the animal and took it to a local veterinarian, who confirmed it had been assaulted. (The animal was eventually killed because of its injuries.) Following this, the police contacted the protection agency because they feared for the safety of the man's children.

A joint investigation of all the K children was undertaken the following week by both the police and the protection agency. In the initial interviews all the children denied having been sexually assaulted by their father. While the children denied the allegations verbally to both police and the protection agency, the only son showed signs of clinical depression and dissociation, as well as social withdrawal, fearfulness, and anxiety, which led the social work investigator to believe this child had been a victim of the father. The boy was subsequently examined by a local physician, who also noticed the dissociation and apparent depression. A full medical exam revealed an absence of the 'wink reflex' (Hobbs & Wynne 1986) and confirmed the social worker's opinion that the father had sexually assaulted his son. The boy continued to deny the assaults.

The mother shared the protection agency's fears regarding the children, and agreed to have several of them taken into the agency's care until she could have a restraining order enforced against her husband. Because the physician was unsure about the diagnosis, she asked that the child be examined by a second physician at a nearby urban hospital, who specialized in cases of child sexual abuse. The boy was examined two weeks later, and this examination was consistent with the previous findings. The boy continued to deny having been assaulted.

On the basis of the child's denial, and after consultation with the crown attorney, the police decided not to lay charges against the father. At the same time, the boy became more trusting of the social work investigator and, because he was out of reach of his father, disclosed that he had indeed been assaulted regularly. His younger sister then confirmed that this was so, and admitted that she too had been victimized. Even though the children described the father's activities very clearly, the police maintained the view that the medical examinations were not adequate and that the children would make poor witnesses.

The child protection agency and the participating physician felt there was enough evidence to proceed against the father; the police and the Crown did not. While the police and the child welfare agency were unsuccessful in establishing a consensus about the handling of the case, the mother refused to have the father back in the family because she understood that this would precipitate a move by the child protection agency to take her children into care. The husband then left Canada, at which point the police informed immigration authorities that they should not readmit Mr K to the country because he was an 'undesirable.'

Problems with the investigative agencies in this case seemed related to the emphasis the police put on what they considered to be 'adequate evidence.' Coupled with the crown attorney's discomfort with the children as witnesses, the lack of evidence blocked the process of bringing the case to trial. The problem addressed here raises the issue identified by Rogers (1990). In his recommendations to the Government of Canada, Rogers suggests that Parliament revise laws governing child sexual abuse prosecutions to permit qualified experts to testify about the characteristics and dynamics of sexual abuse, and to express opinions on the reliability of a child's statements (p. 23).

In summary, coordination efforts involving collaborative investigative procedures linking the activities of police, child welfare workers, and crown attorneys proved to be the most recalcitrant to our efforts to harmonize and render more effective the efforts of the statutory agencies. The difficulties arose out of the differences in service priorities, professional identities and concomitant professional ideologies. While commitment to the goals of coordinated services were generally acknowledged by all participating agencies, sustained effort proved much more difficult to achieve. In the end, close working relationships among the statutory agencies required more resources than those involved wished to provide or were capable of pursuing. For such collaboration to exist between police, child welfare workers, and crown attorneys, there needs to be extensive support at all levels, from the line service provider to the provincial government ministry.

Stage Two: Legal–Investigatory Decision-Making

A challenging time for coordination of services occurs immediately after the completed investigation. That is, when the statutory agencies need to formulate a plan integrating *legal interventions* with *long-term treatment goals*. The primary intention at this stage in the handling of cases was to bring together the statutory agencies involved and create a forum for discussion of each case. We envisioned regular meetings with the social work investigator, the police investigator, the prosecuting attorney, and the probation officer. Figure 3.1 (see p. 39) emphasizes the ideal of a collaborative, interlocking communication between the agencies whose mandate involves protection of the child and maintenance of the law. When planning these meetings, it was hoped that over time the mandated agencies would evolve into a decision-making team whose collaborative legal decisions regarding each case would facilitate synchronous and interconnected legal dispositions and treatment interventions. Such a team would have constituted a key case-planning resource capable of developing pre-sentence assessments that linked specific legal interventions (criminal and family court) to overall treatment objectives. We believed that this in turn would have led to more appropriate court sentencing, which could be associated with a thoughtful treatment plan.

Within the one-year service phase of this project, we were not able to establish consistent, regular meetings of this nature involving all statutory agencies. Regular meetings were held with the CFS social work investigators and the parent support workers. Necessary collaborations between the police, the Crown, and the probation department generally occurred as a direct result of the abuse investigator making contact, frequently on a catch-as-catch-can basis. The most positive aspect of the project's impact in this area was the general acknowledgment by the mandated agencies that collaboration in this important realm of case management was needed. There was a stated commitment by all involved, in both child welfare and criminal justice sectors, to do whatever they could to improve coordination between the courts and the providers of treatment to abused children, perpetrators, and families.

At the conclusion of an investigation, both CFS and police were required to make their respective decisions and inform the families of the outcome. For the protection agency this meant determining whether or not the abuse was 'founded,' and whether a child was in need of protection. For the police it meant determining whether a crime had been committed and, if so, following with a formal charge. Depending on the circumstances of the case, consultation involving CFS with the police and the crown attorney was useful in planning alternative measures for young offenders and making therapy a condition of those measures.

The CFS social work investigator always informed the family about the outcome of the child protection investigation. If a child (or children) were considered in need of protection, the family was informed and a decision made to remediate the situation in consultation with family members. In the majority of cases the protection agency required the family to sign a 'treatment contract' spelling out the agency's view regarding what the family had to do to alleviate the protection worker's concerns. The treatment contracts spelled out in specific detail the required goals of therapy. Generally, the treatment contracts were signed at the completion of an investigation and at the completion of the initial crisis work being done by the PSW with the non-offending parent(s). Further detail on the treatment contract is offered in the next chapter.

Another serious problem that arose during this stage was the lack of synchronization between the criminal court and other agencies. Frequently, an alleged offender was not brought to criminal court until long after a child's initial disclosure, and often after some members of the family had engaged in treatment. Because of this the family experienced a 'second crisis' at the time of the sentencing of the offender, which often led perpetrators engaged in treatment to feel betrayed and punished by the service system. Overall, crown attorneys and judges poorly understood their integral relationship to the overall interagency case-planning effort and showed little comprehension of how their involvement affected long-term progress in the treatment of perpetrators, victims, and their families.

The following case[2] provides an example of the problems that arose when a crown attorney worked independently without ongoing consultation with CFS and a case manager.

---

[2] In this case the CFS investigative worker was Kathryn Levine, with supervision provided by George MacDonald. The parent support worker was Tracy Fedoruk with supervision from Barry Trute. The case manager was Eleanor Chornoboy with supervision from Elizabeth Adkins.

A mentally retarded thirty-year-old adult was alleged to have sexually abused his twelve-year-old female cousin, June. The investigative workers concluded that abuse had occurred and the parent support worker engaged with June's family. The family was coping well and the brief therapy with the PSW focused on supporting June. A mental retardation worker was appointed case manager and initiated therapy with the offender and his family, while also monitoring the progress of June and her family. The worker made good progress in helping the offender to discuss his feelings and to recognize that what he did was wrong. She also started addressing issues of independence with the aim of helping him separate from his family of origin and establish a life of his own with age-appropriate peers. Unfortunately, this process came to an abrupt end when the crown attorney refused to proceed with charges against the offender. The family understood this as societal acceptance that the abuse was not serious and they subsequently lost their motivation to proceed with therapy. The therapy that might have changed their lives drastically (now highly focused on 'looking after' the mentally retarded son) abruptly ended. This is a case where legally-mandated treatment would have been helpful in assisting the offender and his family to make the changes necessary to limit the possibility of recurrence of sexual abuse.

Circumstances were considerably more positive with juvenile offenders because the court allowed more flexibility with juveniles for 'alternative measures;' that is, a program of treatment in lieu of incarceration. In a number of cases the perpetrators were young offenders who were eligible for these alternative measures. Collaboration involving the police, the crown attorney, and the protection agency was frequently used productively within juvenile court to ensure that these young men received mandated treatment. Our experience would suggest a pressing need for similar flexibility in the adult system.

Stage Three: Systemic Treatment of Child Sexual Abuse

Assignment of a case manager to each family in which a sexual abuse disclosure had been made was a basic tenet of the project. Such a person would assume formal responsibility for the coordination of treatment for all members of the family. He or she would function as a connector among all parties involved, coordinating activities of investigative workers through to treatment staff and communicating with all members of the family. In the initial project design it was felt that this person would be instrumental in preventing families from 'falling through the cracks' in service delivery. The case manager, together with the parent support worker, could alleviate the family's sense of getting 'lost' at some point in the investigative or treatment phases of case management.

A number of considerations guided the service coordinator's selection of a case manager. First, the choice was limited to those who had identified themselves in the community treatment network as having a background in family treatment and a willingness to serve as a case manager. At times, this choice was further limited to persons on the list who had an available place on their workload and could accept a case when treatment needed to be initiated.

Parenthetically, we should note that more professionals, from a wide range of human services, accepted this responsibility than was anticipated at the onset of the project. Although there were times when the assignment of a case manager was slightly delayed because of the unavailability of a person to accept the role immediately when required, no case suffered a long delay in the assignment of a case manager during the course of this rural project.

Another consideration was whether the potential case manager had a prior history of service involvement with the family in question. At times this was a facilitating situation, where a family had been involved in child behaviour issues with the potential case manager in the past, and where a position of trust was well established with family members. At times this was a hindering factor, as when the family had known the potential case manager in a child-protection capacity and viewed this person as an agent of the child welfare system. Consideration was also given to the specifics of each case in terms of which agency's mandate was most appropriate. For example, if a case involved aspects of developmental disability, a first option was to assign the case to someone with community mental retardation services.

Once the case manager was assigned, he or she was responsible for formulating a treatment plan with the family and arranging therapy for each member as appropriate. To aid in the selection of therapists, each case manager was provided with a list of professionals in the local geographic area who were willing to work with sexually abused children, offenders, or family members of abused children.

Not surprisingly, case managers tended to choose other workers from their own agency or those whose work they were very familiar with, rather than reach out to treatment providers who were less well-known to them. After treatment providers had been selected for a case, the case manager was responsible for coordinating the treatment by communicating regularly with those providing the treatment services and arranging consultation meetings as needed.

In their capacity as connectors between CFS protection workers and the treatment teams, case managers were responsible for communicating with CFS regarding a family's progress in treatment. This was especially crucial in cases where the children had been apprehended and CFS faced a decision regarding the advisability of returning the children to their homes.

The case manager was responsible for formulating a treatment plan in consultation with the CFS abuse investigator and the service coordinator. Decisions as to which members of the family required individual, group, or dyadic therapy were made and assignment to appropriate therapists took place. At times the case manager took responsibility for the provision of some aspect of the therapy. Once therapists had been secured, the treatment proceeded, with the case manager serving as the central coordinator of the ongoing treatment to each family member.

The case manager's involvement in the process of treatment is more fully considered in the next chapter.

Problems in case manager coordination of treatment services

Although the position of case manager was an essential aspect of coordinated services, it was actually the least widely understood aspect of the project. This became evident in exit interviews with participating service delivery staff. Many expressed a lack of clarity about the role and lines of accountability for case managers. While treatment providers did not wish their clinical work constrained, most would have welcomed more aggressive coordination of the overall treatment process. Much of the confusion seemed to be linked to a lack of clarity regarding issues of professional accountability and practice supervision. The service coordinator felt some reluctance to become involved in directing the activities of the case managers in case they viewed this as an attempt to assume 'therapeutic control' of the case.

It was clear that for the case manager system to work effectively, there must be coordination of the process by someone a step above the case manager administratively. Ideally this would be a major role played by the service coordinator. Case managers as a group would have benefitted from regularly scheduled meetings with the service coordinator. As one participant stated, 'Case management only works if you're accountable to someone and if someone will nudge you if you're not doing your job. Nobody seemed to be clearly responsible for the management of the case managers.'

A second area of difficulty was the conflict between the case manager and the CFS protection workers. There is a need to keep a clear differentiation of duties and tasks, with open communication between those responsible for protection and those responsible for treatment. The case manager's role is to coordinate treatment, not to assure protection, the protection worker's role is to ensure a child's safety, not to oversee treatment. Protection workers often expressed frustration that case managers did not hold enough meetings with them and that collaborative plans were not always established, creating a vacuum that the protection worker felt obligated to fill. This likely occurred as a direct result of the service coordinator's lack of persistence in making case managers more responsible for the overall coordination of services for each of their cases.

A third area of concern was the case manager's difficulty in conceptualizing a complete treatment plan that considered the needs of all members of the family. There was a general tendency to focus concern on one family sub-system or person. For example, if case managers were working intensely with the non-offending parents and victims, they might neglect the needs of the other children in the family or the offender. While some case managers did maintain their 'meta-perspective' or clinical overview of the whole family system, others drifted towards attending to only a sub-system, thereby making ultimate reconstitutive family work that much more difficult to achieve. Again, supervision of each case manager's plans, with increased and routine accountability to the service coordinator, may have alleviated this concern.

Child and Family Services as the Hub of Treatment

The child welfare agency played a central role in the development and implementation of this coordinated service approach for the investigation and treatment of child sexual abuse. Child and Family Services of Central Manitoba was the sponsoring agency in the test area and played an important part in promoting coordinated services in the local community, among professional groups and at provincial departmental levels. The pivotal position of service coordinator was filled by the supervisor of the child and family services team in the test area. Many of the case managers who served project families were child and family services employees.

This approach is in marked contrast to other, proposed models for treatment for child sexual abuse. These models advocate the creation of a specialized treatment resource, separate from the protection agency, which would provide therapeutic services to the families (e.g., Giaretto 1982; Larson & Maddock 1986). We, however, felt it strategic to employ CFS agencies as the central hub of the community services, for several reasons. First, the rural context set tight parameters on the availability of resources specifically for the treatment of sexually abused children, the perpetrators of the violence, and the family members of victims. Sparse local treatment resources needed to be employed in a thoughtful, efficient manner to maximize their benefits. Although the CFS agency in a rural area is not often the sole provider of treatment services to children and their family members, rural communities most often associate them with services to abused children. Further, they clearly hold the mandate for *protection* of children, and must be directly involved in any decision relating to the safety and well-being of children in the community they serve. As well, the CFS has credibility as coordinator of special community services for children, because it is generally viewed in rural communities as the agency responsible for taking care of children. For these reasons it was important to ensure that those with child welfare authority played an active role in our coordinated service model.

We will now carefully examine the practical and political viability of using Child and Family Services as the central hub of a community-based child sexual abuse treatment system. Advantages and disadvantages of such a model will be considered.

Child and Family Services as a treatment resource

The central issues that arise with regard to utilizing a protection agency as a treatment resource are twofold: (1) whether one agency can meet both protection and therapeutic needs of the family; and (2) whether one worker can function, at different times and with different families from the same rural community, as both investigative worker and therapist.

Child and Family Services of Central Manitoba had used a specialized model of service delivery previously, in the early 1980s. This model was unique in the Province of Manitoba in that the agency had already tailored its broad child welfare mandate to include specialized jobs with distinct responsibilities: child abuse investigator (a role that dealt with abuse and protection issues in the broadest sense); family services treatment worker (family counsellors in the broadest sense); foster home coordinator, single-parent and permanent-ward worker; and adoption worker. Thus, within this particular agency, social workers could not, as a matter of service policy, simultaneously occupy both statutory and therapeutic roles. Along with this functional specialization, the agency interpreted its mandate under child welfare legislation as including *both* protection and treatment. Service responsibilities were taken very seriously in both realms.

The agency's impetus to move from generic to specialized social work arose out of a number of fundamental considerations. In the early 1980s a large number of agency personnel began to become interested in the 'family systems perspective,' especially as it pertained to seriously abusive and neglectful families. The agency established family-systems practice as a priority in training for its workers. At the same time, there was a general recognition within the agency that there were large numbers of seriously disturbed families in the community that were not receiving counselling services from other agencies because they were considered the responsibility of the child welfare agency. These were the families normally regarded as 'difficult to engage' or 'involuntary,' and who usually came to the attention of the local human service network because they were subject to statutory child protection orders.

Having accepted the role of therapist as clearly delineated within child welfare legislation, and recognizing the dearth of counselling services available to such families, the agency described its workers as either abuse investigators or family treatment staff. In other words, a worker could not be both simultaneously. Workers discovered very quickly that they could not investigate a family and implement a protection order one week and the next week inform the same family that they would be functioning as neutral, non-judgmental therapists. Such 'role gymnastics' were complicated enough for professional social workers to maintain, and they were impossible when dealing with chaotic families under severe stress. The abuse assessment undertaken by a child welfare investigator began to be regarded as a first and strategic step in intervening with families who would not normally avail themselves of therapy. The next step after a legal – investigatory involvement, was to assign the case to a more 'neutral' family worker who focused on the overall well-being of the family rather than solely on child protection issues.

In contrast to this point of view, some professionals take the position that it is possible, even preferable, to combine the social control and treatment roles or have one worker involved with the family throughout the investigation and treatment process. They cite two basic advantages: (1) the family is not required to relate their story over and over again to different professionals; (2) having one worker can make case planning and the delivery of services more consistent (Carroll 1978; Meddin & Hansen 1985). Some social workers view treatment as beginning with the investigation phase, and argue that it is at this crisis point that positive change in family functioning can be most effectively pursued.

While there is controversy in the literature about separating abuse investigation and treatment roles, the child protection agency in our test area had previously committed itself to separate specialized social work roles. This was consistent with the coordinated treatment approach we followed, which is based on a clear division between the two service roles (i.e., that it is unwise and perhaps impossible for one person to be both the agent of social control and the treatment provider).

Larson and Maddock (1989) argue that it is important to differentiate the duties of 'enforcers' and 'healers' in the provision of child sexual abuse services. Bedford (1983) would agree that there is often conflict between the responsibilities of a therapist and those of a statutory worker. The general belief behind this argument is that the expectations of a protection worker's role are in direct conflict to those of a therapist. Such conflict is seen as interfering with the ability of the worker to establish a trusting, therapeutic relationship with the family, thus hampering its ability to make positive changes. Further, Berliner (1988) argues that investigative interviewing and therapeutic interviewing are two distinctly different skills. Helfer and Schmidt (1976) suggest that highly specialized roles need to be maintained in child abuse services; for example, that one professional provides *crisis* services while another works with a family in *long-term* treatment.

In designing this project we knew that the role of the protection agency would be fundamental to its overall positive outcome, and we considered ourselves fortunate to be working with an agency where specialization ensured clearly differentiated roles. We did think it possible for the same professionals to provide different kinds of services to different families, but only as long as there was absolute clarity about the boundaries of each. It was our premise that treatment services have a legitimate place within a child welfare setting. While we wanted to see this treatment base expanded to other agencies in the area, we viewed Child and Family Services as the appropriate human service agency to act as the 'traffic cop' or central coordinator, thereby serving as the hub of the service system that would respond to situations of child sexual abuse.

Advantages of Child and Family Services as the hub of treatment

Many advantages emerged from the above-mentioned strategy. Child welfare agencies in rural Canadian communities are mandated to provide both protection and treatment for families in which children are deemed to be at risk for neglect and abuse. Therefore, there is little resistance, from both administration and line workers in the child welfare agency, to giving priority to families in which an allegation of sexual abuse has been made. (Such resistance is more common in agencies that hold no such mandate.)

All disclosures of child sexual abuse must, by law, be reported to a child and family services agency in Manitoba. In some families the evidence of abuse is clear and the family can be directed into treatment, through either criminal or family court. There are, however, many cases where the evidence of abuse is unclear. For example, a victim may recant his or her story, or victims may be too young for their evidence to be accepted in court. In many of these instances the child welfare protection workers have a strong sense that something has occurred, but are unable to attain sufficient evidence to proceed to court. Through their efforts with some families, treatment is initiated with family members even though the case is not proceeding to trial. Through their access to family court, child welfare personnel can bring to bear on behalf of children some functional 'judicial leverage' that is not as readily available to those working in other human service settings.

When the service coordinator's position (the position at the centre of the hub and the ultimate overseer of the functioning of the entire service system) is held by a supervisor of the child welfare unit involved in providing investigative and treatment services, many advantages for overall community coordination are created. By the very nature of his child welfare position, the service coordinator in our project had knowledge of every case that came to the attention of the CFS agency. He had close, regular contact with the child welfare protection workers and was involved in case planning right from the beginning. Someone with experience in child and family services is also well suited to be a service coordinator in a coordinated services system, because he or she already understands both the protective and treatment issues involved in child sexual abuse. In overseeing the service delivery pattern in response to child sexual abuse, it is important to understand the roles of the various professional groups and to promote understanding between the service sectors. Professionals who have never been involved in the investigative side of this kind of abuse often cannot fully understand the key service elements inherent in the abuse investigator's role.

When investigative and treatment workers are employed by the same agency, chances for coordination and communication are enhanced. The workers frequently share office space and meet regularly at team meetings, agency meetings at a central office, or for routine agency activities. All workers are exposed to the same training opportunities (e.g., Child and Family Services of Central Manitoba arranged regular consultations with a senior clinician and a family therapist from a nearby city). They were thus more likely to hold a shared treatment ideology and to experience fewer conflicts in case management. There was also significantly less chance of investigative workers undermining therapeutic interventions (Woodard & Woodard 1983) because all investigative workers in this project had received basic training in family-focused social work practice and were clear about their own service roles in such situations.

During the course of the project, communication among the workers from the participating CFS agency steadily increased as protection and treatment efforts were better synchronized. It was clear that this internal, within-agency communication was more intense than it had been in the past (prior to implementation of the coordinated model) and was occurring more frequently than was the case with workers in the comparison CFS agency. Over the time period of the project, we observed that staff turnover was lower and staff morale higher in the child welfare team participating in the test area than they were in the comparison area team. We hypothesize that the more positive staff circumstances in the child welfare agency in the test area were directly related to the increased levels of collaborative team functioning in that agency. These observations are consistent with the research of Fryer et al. (1988), who surveyed child protection units across the United States. Their findings showed more positive attitudes towards work when staff could work as members of a team. Peer support provided by fellow workers was found to reduce levels of job stress. When the rural child welfare agency is centrally involved in coordinated investigative and treatment services for sexually abused children, it does seem to have immediate advantages. Workplace stress is reduced and staff morale, particularly for child welfare investigative workers, is heightened.

Disadvantages of Child and Family Services as the hub of treatment

While placing child welfare services at the hub of coordinated community services had many advantages, there were also clear disadvantages to this arrangement. Some child welfare workers found it difficult to maintain 'therapeutic neutrality' (i.e., a non-judgmental and non-punitive perspective in the process of healing). While child welfare workers providing clinical treatment services were aware that their overriding mandate was to protect children, this awareness did interfere sometimes with their ability to function effectively as therapists for a family. This is not surprising. Workers in a child welfare agency are continually confronted with extreme cases of abuse. They, probably more than anyone else in society, see on a daily basis the emotional injury that abuse wreaks on children. They, as representatives of the agency that may become the guardian of the abused children, must deal with the extreme difficulties these children face as they strive to overcome a history of abuse. The question arises as to whether 'therapeutic neutrality' is the best position to take in such situations. Too many times, professionals who do not experience the initial trauma of an abused child tend to minimize the seriousness of the effects on the child. On the other hand, a child or parent dealing with a CFS worker may feel restricted and unsafe, concerned that everything they say may be used to assure protection of the children; that is, that what they disclose to a child welfare worker may lead ultimately to removal of that child from the family.

As we have stated, a basic tenet of this project was to clearly separate protection and treatment roles. Having the CFS agency as the hub of treatment could turn into a disadvantage. For example, the frequent communication between the CFS protection worker and the CFS family service treatment worker occasionally resulted in blurred service boundaries. At times it influenced assigned treatment workers and weakened their resolve to maintain the clinical stance of therapeutic neutrality. Frequent supervision, ongoing consultation, and education can address these difficulties when child welfare workers are aware of this central issue. A rule was made and enforced in the coordinated services approach that child welfare investigators should not talk about their investigatory activities with (or even within earshot of) an assigned case therapist.

Although there were advantages, there were also inherent difficulties created by having a supervisor from the child welfare agency function as the service coordinator as well. The major flaw was the blurring of the duties of CFS supervisor and service coordinator. In particular, CFS workers were sometimes unclear as to the specific service capacity in which the service coordinator was functioning. For example, the service coordinator might attend a case management meeting as the supervisor of the CFS agency in order to present and support the child and family services' view of the protection issues involved with a particular family. This role compromised his ability to be regarded as an independent coordinator of treatment across all agencies. As one worker stated, 'It's hard to figure out what he is and what hat he's wearing. Is he a colleague? supervisor? project worker?'

A fundamental problem with the role of service coordinator as it emerged in this project was the lack of formal authority to deal with decisions made by different agencies involved in each abuse case. In developing an effective coordinated approach it is important that each participating agency feel a sense of ownership in the process. However, in this case, formal lines of authority within the coordinated services system needed to be more formally delineated. Treatment providers needed to be clearly accountable to a case manager, and case managers needed to be clearly accountable to a service coordinator.

Having one agency (in this case the CFS agency) serve as the hub of treatment did seem to lessen the feelings of ownership in workers from other community agencies. This became very clear in exit interviews in which several workers from other community agencies said they felt this project was largely a child welfare venture.

A retrospective view

In retrospect we believe that the advantages of having the CFS agency serve as the hub of treatment outweighed the disadvantages. We would recommend maintaining this basic element in the coordinated service model with a clear separation of protection and treatment roles. We would however, recommend *against* having a senior CFS staff person function as the service coordinator *within their usual scope of duties* for the reasons elaborated on earlier. This position could be seconded from child welfare or mental health departments, or another allied human service agency, but would be best *jointly funded* by the departments of family services, health, and justice. This would ensure the creation of an independent coordinator of the local service network who was not solely 'owned' by, or who had their major service commitment with, any one community agency.

Helfer and Schmidt (1976) argue that a person in a pivotal role such as that of service coordinator should *not* be an expert in the field of child abuse but should be identified as a facilitator and coordinator. They expressed the view that, 'If she is seen as a child-abuse-and-neglect expert by the community, she may lose her ability to coordinate and become a threat to some agencies or individuals' (p. 249). Our experience in rural communities would challenge this view. We found that it was vital for the coordinator to appreciate all aspects of investigation and treatment, so that informed advice and questioning could ensure the complex responses that are necessary in child sexual abuse services. It is true that having a central coordinator of services with child welfare affiliations will threaten or challenge some agencies and service providers. The issue then becomes: How does one proceed to deal with, and positively resolve and prevent, the occasional surfacing of these professional discomforts or rivalries. In the maintenance of effective and coordinated

community service systems, the need to deal with power issues between professionals is just as critical as it is within families in which
incest has occurred.

The Coordinated Community Service Model: An Overview

Our intent has been to identify and highlight essential service components of a coordinated service model to respond to child sexual
abuse in rural communities. This approach involves the drawing
together of local agencies in a shared, collaborative planning process
that is based on the premise that coordinated services must be implemented, monitored, and maintained by line-level service providers. These are the key actors in such integrated systems. Further,
commitment needs to be developed at the senior administration level
of each of the participating agencies, be it child welfare, mental
health, or police. These administrators can sanction and support
the efforts of their line staff, or they can sabotage interagency activities through the tightening of resources or the limiting of staff
participation (e.g., through maintaining too-large case-loads or prohibiting the travel necessary to attend collaborative community planning meetings).

At a higher political level, it is also important to secure support
from the provincial government to ensure that interdepartmental
bridging is created which facilitates key policy elements. Such elements would include investigatory guidelines that require interdisciplinary assessments or that identify child sexual abuse as a service
priority that warrants departmental attention (e.g., that child sexual
abuse is a legitimate mental health issue that deserves the involvement of the Department of Health, or that it is a high-priority criminal justice issue that should be given special attention by crown
attorneys in the Department of Justice). The design of a coordinated
treatment system needs political support most profoundly at the
grass roots of local communities. However, this support also must
be developed at various points of authority – from the local rural
community all the way up to senior departmental levels in
government.

At the local community level, it seems clear that three fundamental components need to be created for a coordinated service
system: a community treatment committee, a service coordinator,
and case managers. First, a community treatment committee needs

to be formally structured to provide a forum for community service planning by participating agencies. It is within the scope of the community treatment committee to provide opportunities to share and understand differing professional ideologies with regard to the handling of child sexual abuse situations. It functions as a vehicle for formal case reviews and for the evolution of a service system in which community professionals understand how patterns of collaborative investigation and treatment can best be maintained in their local area. It is a useful structure for the provision of training and supervision in areas in which there is heightened local need.

It is vital in a coordinated system to have one person identified as the local traffic cop for all identified cases of child sexual abuse. This person is the service coordinator, who has formal responsibility for seeing that there is a planned and smoothly functioning bridge between those who do the investigative work and those who can provide treatment services. The service coordinator ensures that the community treatment committee meets regularly to maintain interagency communication and service collaboration. The service coordinator assigns a case manager for each case of child sexual abuse and monitors the work of each case manager.

Although practice supervision for individual treatment workers is provided by their home agency according to its standards and protocols, the case manager must monitor each case to be sure each treatment provider is meeting his or her commitments within a systematic treatment strategy. This means that all abused children have comprehensive treatment plans involving them and their family members, and that treatment is delivered in a thoughtful, sequential manner that is appropriate to the circumstances of each case of child sexual assault.

Each treatment plan is developed by balancing what a case requires with the resources that can be secured in the home community. In our experience, this called for local caregivers to try to meet high priority needs with very limited resources. It then led to the creation of new local resources such as group treatment for both victims and juvenile perpetrators in order to maximize what were slim treatment resources in the rural communities.

Much responsibility for the maintenance of a collaborative approach during the treatment phase rests in the hands of individual case managers. This can be both a strength and a weakness in the coordinated model. Its strength is that each case has someone who is responsible for tracking the progress of the case and ensuring that services are being provided according to a systemic treatment plan. Its weakness lies in the level of commitment and energy of each case manager and his or her willingness to provide service in the best interest of the client.

Interdisciplinary boundaries can be most sensitive when decisions are made regarding service delivery. It was during the treatment phase that it was most important to maintain high interdisciplinary congruence with regard to a shared ideology of treatment. Because most treatment providers shared a 'family systems view' concerning intervention, collaborative case planning was more readily achieved. Because most treatment providers appreciated the need for sequential and multi-modal therapies (e.g., individual counselling, group sessions, dyadic interventions, and family therapy), there were few professional skirmishes over treatment plans. The challenge seemed to be not so much the putting together of a shared strategy of intervention as finding the basic clinical resources necessary to adequately help abused children and their family members.

It is important to recognize that the coordinated model will inherently mean periods of heightened anxiety and stress in professionals as the system is being created and implemented. The collaborative approach can bring immediate benefits to individual professionals working in rural locales. Rural professionals value the emotional and practical support such shared work can bring from their peers. They appreciate the potential professional growth offered by close collaboration with other caregivers. However, there is heightened stress associated with the close scrutiny of others. Being responsible to others who function outside of one's home agency for the work one does, and for the quality of one's professional practice, can be frightening. It seems as well that workers in the child sexual abuse service area frequently have unrealistic expectations regarding the ability of families to change, or in the speed in which change will come. When a family fails to change, workers may feel 'exposed, inadequate and angry' (Fletcher 1982).

When planning and building such coordinated service systems, one needs to anticipate times of high professional anxiety and reactivity. The community treatment committee is a vital aspect of the model in this regard, because it gives participants a structured setting in which they can voice their concerns, attitudes, and perceptions.

Each community will have its own unique mix of professional resources, agency structures, and socio-cultural realities. We have acknowledged that one cannot devise a blueprint for coordinated services in response to child sexual abuse that will meet every community's needs. We have attempted, however, to offer key strategic elements in this chapter that could serve to guide individualized planning efforts in each unique community setting.

4

Early Crisis Intervention in Child Sexual Abuse Services

A disclosure of child sexual abuse often triggers a complex response, within and outside the boundaries of a family in which incest has occured. The disclosure will pull human-service agencies, responsible for the protection of children and the maintenance of law and order in the community, directly into the life of the family. Many human-service sectors, spanning child welfare, police, medical care, and mental health, claim some jurisdiction in the field of child sexual abuse. Child welfare agencies and police are directed by government legislation to investigate any allegation of assault on a child. Often treatment services that could ameliorate the trauma associated with such abuse are delayed pending confirmation that the allegation is substantiated. Because of the complexity of such situations, the investigative process can be lengthy, confusing, and extremely difficult for victims and their families.

Professionals involved in different aspects of the investigation can work at cross purposes, with different priorities and perspectives on the situation. Child welfare personnel are mandated to ensure the physical safety and psychological well-being of the child. Police are mandated to investigate violations of the law and to ensure that adequate evidence is collected to meet the needs of the criminal justice system. These different mandates can create a powerful intrusion into the lives of children and their families, when different professionals inquire in a repetitive, seemingly uncoordinated manner. Outsiders asking questions are seen to invade the life of the family. For victims there may be multiple interrogations that can weaken their resolve to provide evidence of abuse and make them feel more vulnerable as family tension increases. For some children the trauma associated with the investigative process can be more acute than the trauma associated with the sexual abuse (Schultz 1973). In incestuous situations, victims want the abuse to stop but many do not want to lose their family as they know it as the ultimate price of sexual safety.

A situation in which there is an allegation of intrafamilial abuse or assault by a trusted adult in the life of a child, such as a babysitter or family friend, represents a serious crisis that unbalances and threatens the stability of a family. In most cultures and communities child sexual abuse is a shame-laden act that depends on the domination and silence of victims. When the silence is not maintained and the secret is disclosed, a range of family responses can occur. Family members may not believe the victim because of the serious ramifications of the situation. At times the alleged perpetrator is protected for fear of the disintegration of the family. It is a situation that challenges the boundaries of family loyalty and forces difficult choices in terms of family alliances and emotional bonds (Gelinas 1983).

Unfortunately, most victims and their non-offending parents are left in a state of legal limbo while the investigative process is conducted. Often mental health treatment is withheld pending the disposition of the investigation. If litigation seems imminent, many parents will protect their legal position and what they see as their family's best interests by curtailing or entirely avoiding discussion of the abuse with human service professionals attempting to provide services. In the short term, too few children and their families receive counselling or help with key intimate relationships in their life, to help them cope with the social and psychological consequences of the disclosure of sexual abuse.

We have previously identified two fundamental family crises triggered by disclosure of sexual assault on a child. The first is the challenge to the stability of interpersonal relationships within the family and the part played by the abuse in altering these relationships. Fundamental here is the message that parents in this family do not protect their children, thus creating a situation where the children have become vulnerable to 'attack trauma' from within the family and cannot feel safe. This is a crisis based on an internal threat to family stability. The second crisis is based on an external threat to the continued existence of the family's current structure and composition. Here, the intrusion of what are often seen as hostile outsiders, who have the potential to change the family by removing one or more of its members, create 'institutional trauma.' Both crises can be toxic to the family. How family members cope with them can have a profound effect on the future well-being of the victim, the alleged perpetrator, and all other members of the family.

There are several aspects of traditional crisis intervention theory (Caplan 1964; Rapoport 1962) that are highly salient to the circumstances of child victims and their families. Crisis intervention theory informs us that focused and immediate services are needed to assist victims of crisis situations. It is understood that people in crisis are often more psychologically open to outside help in resolving toxic circumstances that seem beyond their control (Golan 1978; Brockopp 1973). Unfortunately, in many child sexual abuse situations, the prolonged investigative period can result in a protracted state of 'institutional trauma,' in which victims may be related to as family scapegoats or cast aside as family members recoil from the tension and confusion they associate with professionals disrupting the stability and security of their family. Many families totally close themselves to the outside world, becoming 'emotional fortresses.' This circumstance makes it particularly hard for mental health practitioners to reach those families to provide the long-term treatment that is frequently required in cases of child sexual abuse.

Non-offending Parents as Primary Recipients of Crisis Services

The non-offending parent can play a pivotal role as the 'gatekeeper' of the family. Non-offending parent in this instance refers to a mother or father who is seen by investigators as not being actively involved in the sexual abuse or having colluded in its secrecy. In instances of intrafamilial sexual abuse, the majority of non-offending parents are mothers. When a child is sexually assaulted, by a family member or by another trusted adult, the mother often holds the key position in the recovery process both for the victim and for the family as a whole. Affective support, especially from a parent, serves to buffer a child against life stress (Rutter 1975). However, the disclosure of sexual abuse is different from other family crises. Here the mother is often asked to resolve immediately any conflict she may feel between obligations she holds for the victim and obligations she holds for the alleged perpetrator, be it her husband or son (Gelinas 1983; James & Nasjleti 1983).

Responses by mothers to disclosures of incestuous assaults on their children are complex and diverse. They range from being supportive to denying the abuse, and can involve collusion, knowledge without action, or total lack of awareness. The important point is that, in situations where mothers have not actively participated or condoned the sexual abuse, they simply cannot be held responsible for the act itself. Whatever their reason for not attending to warning signs in the family, if indeed such signs existed, they will be under a great deal of stress at the time of the disclosure. In incest-related crisis situations, a mother is expected to act quickly and decisively to ensure that her child does not endure further harm. At a time when her own social, psychological, and economic stability may be at risk, she needs to respond to a highly complex and emotionally charged event that will have profound long-term implications for the victim's well-being, for her future relationship with the alleged perpetrator, and for the long-term survival of her family. At the time of disclosure, victims of child sexual abuse need a great deal from family members, particularly from a non-offending parent. They need to be believed, to trust that they will not be abandoned, and to be assured that they will be protected from further exploitation and abuse. They need to know that they are not responsible for the crisis in the family. This is a great deal to expect from a parent who is in a state of crisis herself.

Many factors will come into play in a mother's response to the sexual victimization of one or more of her children. Byerly (1985) suggests that non-offending mothers are often dealing with many other personal and social difficulties, such as low self-esteem and isolation from social networks, which impede their ability to help victimized children. If the mother is herself a victim of sexual abuse, then her own unresolved issues may limit her emotional support to her victimized child. In such situations, it is important to help the mother begin to deal with her own history of trauma. In the short term, this needs to happen to the extent that the mother can begin to recognize the realities of her child's victimization without projecting her own unresolved issues into her child's situation. Even when a mother who was blind to the incest acts expeditiously to protect her victimized child, she will invariably feel she has failed as a parent. She will believe she has failed to give her victimized child the protection she should have been providing.

Some children find that, when they break the silence and disclose the secret of their sexual molestation, they are disbelieved by their mother, the person they may most depend upon to end the abuse. Such negative parental reactions to the disclosure heighten the trauma for the child. If the mother disbelieves or blames the child, the victim's problems of self-blame and guilt are further compounded by feelings of betrayal and rejection. Recent studies have confirmed that lack of maternal support following a disclosure of incest is associated with higher psychopathology in the child (Everson, Hunter, Runyon, Edelsohn, & Coulter 1989; Adams-Tucker, C. 1982).

To protect the victim from long-term deleterious effects of sexual abuse and to reduce the potential of the family recoiling from institutional trauma, immediate short-term crisis services should be routinely available for non-offending parents in situations of intrafamilial child sexual abuse (Rivera 1988). It is our experience that these services can reduce psychological distress in non-offending parents, prepare the family to be more open to long-term mental health services, and help the family to be less reactive to the intruding investigative and judicial processes.

Implementation of the Parent Support Service

A special crisis service was created to help bridge the investigative procedures and treatment services required when disclosures of intrafamilial and trusted-third-party abuse were received by child welfare authorities. Consistent with the definition of intrafamilial abuse employed in the overall project, this type of abuse was defined for the Parent Support Service as including sexual assaults by members of the nuclear family (e.g., sibling, father) or extended family (e.g., uncle, cousin), as well as those identified as a trusted third parties, such as babysitters, teachers, or clergy.

The Parent Support Service essentially employed an "independent" counsellor, the parent support worker (PSW), who was not directly responsible either to the police or to child welfare authorities. This role was seen as that of a mental health counsellor, and two of the three PSWs in our project were on the staff of community mental health agencies. A primary objective of the service was to assist family members, in particular non-offending parents, to cope with the immediate crisis events that challenged the stability of the family unit. As quickly as possible after a disclosure of child sexual abuse, an appointment was made to do individual counselling with the non-offending parent – most often the mother. In cases of sibling incest, assault by trusted third parties or extended family members, both mothers and fathers were offered service. On average, parents were seen on a weekly basis for six to eight sessions. This chapter offers a review of the most salient practice themes that emerged from the Parent Support Service.[1]

Key Practice Elements

The first duties of a PSW were to establish an atmosphere of trust with each non-offending parent, to strengthen the immediate psychological and social coping resources of non-offending parents, to ensure safety and support for victims in their homes, and to facilitate functional family adjustment to the circumstances associated with the disclosure of child sexual abuse. In the short term, the service was meant to ease the level of situational stress on non-offending family members and reduce further sexual, physical, or psychological victimization of the abused children. The following are key practice elements identified as being most salient in the process of service delivery.

Parents' Subjective Interpretation of the Disclosure Crisis

The worker has to determine immediately whether the mother and family are truly 'in crisis.' If so, he or she must determine which factors are perceived as threatening, which are not being resolved, and which are maintaining the crisis state. A thorough exploration is required at the onset concerning what non-offending parents perceive as the most threatening elements of the disclosure situation. This analysis usually provides information about the parents' cognitions relating to the child abuse, their coping responses and re-

---

[1] All case vignettes in this chapter are drawn from the practice of Tracy Fedoruk and Gloria Vaughan-Jones, who served as parent support workers while completing their MSW degrees. Barry Trute provided primary supervision to both practitioners.

sources, and the specific stressors that challenge their personal well-being and the well-being of the victim and other family members. The following case study exemplifies this practice issue:

Mrs Anderson's thirteen-year-old daughter disclosed that while visiting her father (separated from the family) she was sexually abused by him, and had been for a number of years. John, Mrs Anderson's common-law husband of three years, talked with the PSW about the stress that the previous two weeks (since the disclosure) had brought to his relationship with Mrs Anderson: 'We are no longer talking about things, and when we do talk it is all about the abuse. I feel like I'm shutting down. I am finding ways to keep myself busy so I won't have to talk about it. I feel like I can forget about it momentarily while I'm at work but often feel overwhelmed by the burden of coming home.'

The PSW helped John see his reaction as similar to that of many people when shocking things happen in their lives. 'Initially, they feel they can talk or think about nothing else, and the shocking event becomes all absorbing. The tendency to avoid talking about it, or situations which remind them about it, is a natural one.' The worker also helped Mrs Anderson and her partner discuss what the abuse had meant emotionally to each of them, and what it meant to the ongoing circumstances in the life of their family. She encouraged them to try and go on with their lives for now, and to trust that things would improve with time. She acknowledged that there was a risk of believing that this disrupted home situation was the way things were going to be 'for the rest of your life.' She helped them talk to one another about how some things will change, and how some things will need to be changed, as a result of the daughter's disclosure of sexual abuse.

For some families, the sexual abuse in and of itself does not represent a crisis event in their lives. Their crisis state is more largely tied to institutional trauma; that is, to the intrusion of the outside world threatening to break the family apart, through the apprehension of children or the incarceration of the perpetrator. Consider the following case:

While meeting with the PSW, mother expressed a great deal of anger toward the investigative social worker from the child welfare agency. Despite the mother's willingness to allow the agency to apprehend her daughter temporarily, she was disturbed by its abrupt handling of the situation and felt her status as guardian had been undermined. The agency had taken her daughter away from the hospital immediately following a medical examination without informing her, and she was unaware of her child's whereabouts or emotional state. All of this had occurred though the father, the alleged perpetrator, no longer resided in the home and the daughter's safety was not threatened there. The mother also felt the agency blamed her for the abuse that had been perpetrated by her husband. When she asked the social worker from the child welfare agency why he thought her daughter didn't tell her about the abuse, he reportedly responded, 'Perhaps you were not very close to your daughter.'

Attempting to gather information from the child welfare worker, her daughter's physician, and a mental health consultant who had been involved, the mother made numerous telephone enquiries, most of which were not returned. When these professionals did respond, the information given was vague, leaving the mother feeling blamed, distrusted, and misunderstood. She also felt that the professionals perceived her inquiries as intrusive rather than as a sign of the genuine caring of a mother for her daughter.

The PSW attempted to validate this mother's anger. She acknowledged that feelings of being blamed and self-blame are tied to some of the most difficult emotions mothers in these situations have to deal with. She also acknowledged that incest often involves great secrecy, making it difficult sometimes for mothers to know such behaviour is going on in their own families. She comforted the mother by assuring her that outsiders often do not understand the power of this secrecy, and that they tend to blame the mother for allowing the abuse to happen. In this instance the PSW could tell the mother that she accepted the truth of her story, that she had been unaware of the abuse and shocked by what had happened. She then helped the mother consider alternative ways to deal with the professionals involved in her daughter's life. She encouraged her to continue to exercise her right to seek information from the community agencies in order to remain an active, supportive parent to her daughter.

Many parents will need assistance in planning how best to deal with the professionals who require information from them, their victimized child, and the alleged perpetrator. Once such information has been gathered, these professionals will often withhold information as to what is happening during the course of the investigation and what is likely to happen if the allegation is substantiated. The PSW can assist parents to gain information from police and from child protection workers. This will reduce the parents' stress and feelings of vulnerability that stem from not knowing what is being decided about their children and families by those in authority.

In most instances, the sexual assault and the institutional response to the assault will weave together to upset the fragile stability of the family in which incest has occurred. However, any immediate crisis intervention treatment needs to be anchored in the client's subjective interpretation of what constitutes a threat to her well-being and the stability and safety of the family.

Establishment of the Role and Purpose of the Parent Support Worker

A first clinical challenge for a PSW is to take a stance of 'judgment neutrality,' which means in this context that support workers should communicate on initial contact that they are not in a position to judge whether or not the alleged assault occurred, because they are not in a position to gather evidence or determine guilt. This 'judgment neutrality' is complementary to the family therapy technique of 'multilaterality' in treating intrafamilial child sexual abuse (Gelinas 1986). Multilaterality refers to the actions taken by the therapist to ensure that all family members, including the perpetrator of the abuse, feel their interests are recognized and that they will be given a fair hearing in the process of family therapy. Judgment neutrality refers to the preliminary stance taken by a PSW not to be aligned with the investigative agencies. However, the PSW should be clear in expressing the conviction that child sexual abuse is wrong and should not be condoned under any circumstance.

In our experience it was important to tell the parents that any information that related to additional discoveries or suspicions of child abuse would be reported to the authorities. Apart from such circumstances, the families were assured that whatever was discussed would remain confidential unless the parents gave their written permission for the release of information. In particular, the PSW assured the parents that she would not act as a conduit of information for investigative child welfare personnel or the police. The PSW then had to walk a middle road between the parents and the human service agencies involved. It was important that the support worker was seen by all involved parties as an independent actor who was not aligned, as part of the investigative process, on the side of the parents or on the side of the community agencies.

As our project proceeded, the parent support workers clearly and directly indicated that they were not an agent of the police or the child welfare agency who were doing 'the investigative job they had to do.' It was important for the PSWs to emphasize that their primary function was to counsel and assist the non-offending parent. It was important to state to parents who claimed that the allegation of child sexual abuse was false that, even if the allegation of child sexual abuse was not true, the family was in crisis because of the disclosure. It was also acknowledged that any family would be upset by these powerful circumstances. The worker offered to be a resource to help the non-offending parent decide what to do to stabilize her family and plan for the future well-being of her children given the reality that a disclosure of sexual abuse had been made. This indication of service parameters was a relief to most parents and a welcome aid. Most did not have anyone in their life who would be there 'just for them' during this time of crisis.

Assessing the Victim-Parent Relationship: Issues of Belief and Blame

In the following example, an early assessment was completed by the PSW as to the parent's knowledge regarding the alleged abuse. Central to this was the importance of determining whether the parent believed the victim's allegations.

Mrs Brown initially stated she did not believe her daughter Sandy's disclosure that her husband had sexually assaulted Sandy. The mother said she believed her daughter was lying because she was angry with 'house rules.' Further, she said Sandy had a 'bruise on her brain' (a reference to an accidental injury that took place when Sandy was eight years old) that was the cause of her tendency to tell lies.

Instead of directly confronting Mrs Brown's assertions, the PSW emphasized that her concern at this point was not whether the abuse did or did not occur. Rather she was concerned about what it was like for Mrs Brown to be living in a situation in which her daughter had made such allegations against her husband. This initially circumvented the struggle over proving the allegation and created an opportunity for Mrs Brown to talk about her feelings of confusion and her fears for her family. She went on to describe the symptoms of depression she was experiencing and her feeling that she was 'caught in the middle' between her daughter and her husband. Later, she was open to the suggestion by the PSW that it was important to consider what it would mean if Sandy had not lied about the sexual assault. The support worker suggested that sexual abuse was not something children tended to lie about. Mrs Brown explored with the worker what she could do to support her daughter (while not abandoning her husband), if she accepted the idea that her daughter was telling the truth.

Even if the allegation of sexual abuse is accepted by non-offending family members, it is important to assess if the victim is being blamed in any way for the crisis triggered by the disclosure. Children need to know that their mother will protect them and that the incest is not seen as their fault (Sgroi & Dana 1982). A basic task for the support worker is the exploration of the parent's interpretation of what has occurred and what meaning this event has in the life of the family. It is essential that the victim does not serve as the focus of family anger, and that parents appreciate that it is not fair to hold children responsible for the decisions and actions of adults.

Mobilizing the Parent as a Positive Mental Health Resource to the Victim

In most instances it is vital to assist the parent to appreciate what disclosure means to a child, and the child's need to be supported and to know that mother is 'their friend in the family.' At times non-offending parents are ashamed that their victimized children did not tell them about the abuse immediately and directly, as the following case attests:

Mrs Anderson wondered why her daughter Mary had told a teacher at school that she had been sexually abused, instead of coming to her. She felt invalidated by her daughter and blamed by the school. The PSW discussed how difficult it is for children to tell anyone about such abuse. She acknowledged that for some children it is especially difficult to tell their mothers, because their mothers

are the most significant person in their lives. She suggested that it
was because Mary depended on her mother so much that it made it
risky for Mary to tell her.

Children often fear being blamed, misunderstood, or rejected by
their mothers, who may be the only people on whom they most
depend. Some children understand their mother's loyalty (or in some
cases anger) towards the person who abused them, and thus may
feel uncertain how she might react when told about the abuse (Gelinas 1986). The mother should be assisted in every way possible
to show empathy for the victim's distress and to be a strong emotional resource to her victimized child. This often means educating
the mother directly as to how to respond to her child's questions
or needs, sensitizing her to her child's behavioral reactions to the
abuse situation, and helping her devise a thoughtful safety plan
for each victim in the family and for any other child at risk. In
the case of Mary it was important for the PSW to act as a role
model for the mother. Together they prepared answers to the child's
pressing questions and planned specific actions to improve the home
situation.

Many parents of sexually abused children have been sexually
abused during their own childhoods (Faller 1989). In cases such
as the one following, mothers were assisted to contain, focus, and
begin to resolve their own emotional responses to the disclosure
of sexual abuse.

During an interview with Mrs Martin, the PSW explored the intergenerational pattern of abuse that appeared to exist in her family.
Although Mrs Martin had initially contended that she had not been
abused by her father or her brother, it was disclosed that both had
sexually fondled her on numerous occasions. Mrs Martin had not
initially defined these incidents as abuse because they did not 'involve intercourse,' which was her understanding of what constituted sexual abuse. Through the use of family genograms, the PSW
facilitated Mrs Martin's understanding of her own victimization,
increased her sensitivity to her own mother's history of sexual
abuse, and gently explored how her brother might have learned
sexually assaultive behaviours. The worker assisted Mrs Martin to
access long-term treatment in relation to her own victimization,

and explored practical ways that she could provide care for herself (e.g., writing a journal, accepting the support of close friends) in coping with her family difficulties.

Parents who have been victims themselves will often require extensive therapy to come to terms with what happened to them in the past, and to begin to understand how their own victimization has affected their relationship with their partner and children. In our project, parent support workers needed to target their efforts, during the short time period they had with parents, on detoxifying the parent's past personal experiences. In particular, workers had to concentrate on how the parents own victimization was blocking their availability as positive, supportive resources for their children. However, only modest steps can be taken in this regard during crisis intervention work following disclosure.

Moving Beyond Individual Counselling with Parents

The PSW can be of greater assistance if clinical treatment is extended beyond contact solely with the non-offending parent to include conjoint work with the parent and victim. Because of the limited time interval framing this crisis work, it is difficult to provide services that are more widely family-focused. In most cases, short-term crisis counselling will only involve those that are identified as non-offenders and who are in a parental role with the abused child. Clearly no work should be done that brings the victim and perpetrator together without significant preparatory work with both, as well as clear understanding that a meeting will not serve to further abuse the victim.

We concur with the assertion of Sgroi and Dana (1982) that individual therapy with mothers of incest victims is a necessary precursor to involvement in other modalities of therapy. However, if the mother and victim can be seen early after the disclosure in conjoint sessions, clinical treatment can be more powerful. Such intervention, when timed appropriately, creates an opportunity to intervene directly in the transactions between parent and child. This can serve to join the victim and the non-offending parent more closely in a shared understanding of the circumstances of the abuse, and to enhance their positive mutual connectedness to each other through this time of stress and insecurity.

Mrs Trent talked with the worker about concerns that her nine-year-old son John, who had been sexually abused by his father, acted 'as though he were full of evil' and had temper tantrums that 'threw him completely out of control.' The PSW suggested that John's behaviour could be seen as his way of sending a message to his mother that he was in pain and was 'crying for help.' These ideas made sense to Mrs Trent. She admitted that it was difficult for her to talk with her son because 'it meant a new way of relating for the two of them.' The PSW and the mother reflected together on some of the issues that John might be struggling with and discussed what might be said to help John talk about his feelings. The PSW then arranged a series of joint sessions involving the worker, the mother and the son. The worker's intent in the beginning was to support the mother and son as they became more comfortable talking to each other about their feelings. The sexual abuse was not addressed until the mother felt that this 'new way of relating' had begun and that it was emotionally safe, for her and for her son, to address this painful event in their lives.

Incestuous behaviour triggers distress across a family system. It is an issue for every member of the family. In situations involving intrafamilial child sexual abuse, it is important not to ignore the needs of siblings or other extended-family members who may carry confusion and guilt consequent to such a disclosure.

In discussing her three-year-old daughter's sexual abuse, Mrs Davis stated that she did not want her eight-year-old son to know about the abuse because she feared it might lead to incest. She said her son had been asking questions about why the police had been in the home and what had happened to his sister. The PSW suggested to Mrs Davis that incest was dependent on secrecy and that one way to prevent it might be to encourage open communication between family members. She also talked about what might be done to teach children directly about their rights to personal privacy. They both agreed that when children are left to wonder about events in their family, what is imagined is often worse than the reality. Mrs Davis came to appreciate that telling her son about the abuse might help alleviate some of his fears about the situation. The PSW modeled ways of discussing the sexual abuse with an eight-year-old boy and helped the mother plan her own way to discuss this painful issue with her son.

Siblings often have a range of conflicting feelings in response to the sexual abuse of a brother or sister. Whatever feelings siblings have about the abuse, even if they differ from those of other family members, they should be given an opportunity to express them:

Janet Wilson is a single parent of three children: Rob (age 13), Janine (age 11), and David (age 5). Janine recently disclosed that she had been sexually abused by her mother's brother, 'Uncle Don.' The assaults, which included fondling of Janine's breasts and vagina, had taken place while Janet was away from the home for extended periods of time. Apparently these incidents had been occurring over the past several years. In discussions with the PSW, Mrs Wilson expressed concerns that her eldest son's behaviour had become very volatile since Janine's disclosure, and that she was uncertain how to deal with his angry outbursts. The PSW discussed these issues in the context of how difficult it was for siblings and how older brothers may blame themselves for not having protected their younger sisters. The worker also discussed with Mrs Wilson what it would be like to ask her son directly whether or not his uncle had sexually assaulted him. They talked about how Janet might give all the children opportunities to talk about their feelings relating to Janine's disclosure.

Mediating the Relationship Between the Family and the Social Environment

Sexual abuse of a child can leave members of the family feeling fearful and vulnerable even when the perpetrator is a trusted person who is not a member of the immediate household. The following exemplifies the work that must be done to assist parents with neighbourhood or community issues:

Mr and Mrs Johnson live in a small rural community. A neighbour, Louise, had been babysitting the Johnson's four-year-old daughter Sara, since Sara was six months old. The previous summer, Mrs Johnson began hearing from other parents that Sara had been engaging in advanced sex play with boys her own age. A few months later, while sitting on her father's lap, Sara asked her father to 'touch her bum.' Mr and Mrs Johnson questioned their daughter about who was touching her bum. Sara became very upset and disclosed that Louise's seventeen-year-old son had been licking her 'privates' and making her lick and suck his penis. In her contact with the PSW, Mrs Johnson described having gone through an initial period of rage and repulsion towards men, which made it difficult for her to function at work where she had ongoing contact with the public. She also acknowledged feeling increasingly fearful for the safety of her daughter and her own personal safety as well. Because the police were contacted, she feared reprisals from the babysitter's son and family. Mr Johnson described himself as being preoccupied with the situation and having difficulty concentrating at work. He was also afraid of 'losing control over his anger' if he were to come in contact with the alleged perpetrator. Both parents felt stigmatized in their social relations outside of the family.

With the PSW advising and supporting them, the parents began dealing with their crisis immediately following the disclosure. They withdrew their daughter from Louise's care. Both parents established contact with authorities, which included the police and the local child welfare agency, and facilitated a medical examination of their daughter. They secured individual and group treatment for their daughter and enrolled themselves in a support group for parents of victimized children. They discussed with the PSW how they might utilize the informal social support that was available to them from their family and close friends. The PSW explored various options to ensure their own and their daughter's safety. The worker also emphasized how both parents, by believing, supporting, and protecting their daughter, had taken the first and most important steps in helping her to heal.

Parents often fear that their victimized children will be further victimized by the over-reaction of other people in their neighbourhood and community, a reaction that might stigmatize their child and further shame the family. As the following example indicates, the PSW can encourage parents to plan for local reaction and minimize the impact this might have on their child and family:

The Sullivans felt that the impact of the abuse had a detrimental effect on Emily, and they described her as 'clingy' and having tantrums more than usual. Mrs Sullivan described how her daughter had told some children at school about the incident. She worried that her daughter would be teased and possibly ostracized by the other children. Mr and Mrs Sullivan wondered how to deal with this, and how to go about 'street-proofing' Emily and their other two children. The PSW and the Sullivans discussed how the topic might be raised with Emily so that she would learn that even though she did not do anything wrong, there were some things that should be talked about only with family and close friends. The worker suggested it was important for Emily and the other children to express their feelings, and showed the parents how to facilitate this process in the family. Further, the worker offered the parents relevant print materials to help them initiate a dialogue with their children regarding safety.

Many non-offending parents will experience high levels of emotional stress as they anticipate the negative reaction of extended-family members and friends following the disclosure of child sexual abuse. In our experience, families seen for crisis counselling following a disclosure tended to be socially isolated, with sparse social-support networks. These families often appeared enmeshed, and corresponded to the description of Larson and Maddock (1986) as 'closed, highly autonomous' family units with an over-dependence on family members for social support. When these parents identified friends they could turn to for informal social support, it was found that these friendship networks were frequently limited in size and only offered a narrow range of support. Some parents indiscriminately told friends and family members about the disclosure. Others chose not to tell anyone outside the immediate family. Both of these general responses seemed to heighten rather than ameliorate the stress.

Many parents want to tell a close friend or confidante about incidents of child abuse but are unsure of how to do it or what response it will trigger. However, the PSW can assist in the thoughtful release of information and facilitate a planned approach to securing informal social support, as we see here:

Nine-year-old Cathy was adopted shortly after birth by Lori, a single mother with a sixteen-year-old son, Steven, Cathy's stepbrother. Cathy disclosed to Lori that Steven had been sexually abusing her over an extended period of time. Lori herself had a history of sexual abuse in her own family (she resided in a rural community that is geographically distant from members of her family). She was inclined to cope by withdrawing from her friends and associates at work in an attempt to deal with her problems 'behind closed doors.' She feared jeopardizing her role as a professional in the community.

The PSW and Lori reflected together about the circumstances and costs of Lori's withdrawal into social isolation. They talked about the exhaustion Lori was experiencing in looking after all the household chores, child care efforts (including the maintenance of a safety plan for Cathy) and, as well, meeting her professional duties in her workplace. Lori made the decision to share her story with one close friend whom she felt would be sensitive to the family's situation. Discussion ensued as to how she would tell her friend. As well, possible reactions by her friend were anticipated and a plan created to respond to these possible reactions. In a later interview, Lori was pleased to report that she had spoken with her friend, who had responded in a caring, positive manner. Lori requested help with several tasks and chores that were beginning to feel insurmountable. She felt relieved to be able to tell her story to someone other than a professional helper. She found that telling one close friend helped her feel less isolated, less vulnerable, and more hopeful. She felt she had taken important steps to develop a closer, more long-lasting friendship, 'something she had always wished for.'

Conclusions

In ideal circumstances, treatment for children and their families would be initiated immediately following a disclosure of intrafamilial child sexual abuse. Even if the allegation of abuse is unsubstantiated, it is a troubling situation and a signal that all is not well in the life of the family. In most instances, there will be some delay in the initiation of any treatment services for the victim or other family members. In rural locales there can be a prolonged delay caused by an investigative process slowed by travel distances and limited child welfare and police resources. Further, in rural communities treatment resources that are immediately available for child victims and their family members are scarce. These service restrictions can result in prolonged investigations and delayed treatment.

It is important to conceptualize incest as an ecological issue. Larson and Maddock (1986) propose that incest be understood as a reflection of 'boundary disturbances' at four key levels in a family ecosystem: at the boundaries (1) between the family and its social environment, (2) that mark generations of family members, (3) that frame interpersonal relationships between individual family members and (4) that permeate the intrapsychic elements within each family member. A crisis service that seeks to stabilize family functioning in situations of intrafamilial child sexual abuse must address signs of distress that emerge from each of these levels within the family ecosystem.

Short-term crisis counselling services offered immediately following the disclosure of intrafamilial child sexual abuse can be of high utility to non-offending parents. Therapeutic interventions offered in such parent support services are closely consistent with traditional crisis intervention theory. James and Nasjleti (1983) identify this as a 'disclosure-panic' phase of treatment that sets the ground for more extensive, longer-term clinical work with victims and their families. Within this phase of treatment two fundamental crises are seen as requiring focused attention: attack trauma and institutional trauma.

First, the deleterious attack trauma – directly associated with the sexual violation of a child – requires careful intervention. From this perspective, it is important to ensure that children are safe from further attack, that they are not held responsible or blamed for the assault, and that their non-offending parents can serve as a positive mental-health resource to them. Consistent with Faller's assessment (1988) of a maternal caretaker's characteristics, PSWs need to assess a mother's emotional and financial dependence on the perpetrator, her capacity to be loving and nurturing towards her children, and the extent to which she can physically and emotionally protect her children. It is thus important to be able to build a strong relationship with the parents quickly, which will engender their hope and trust in the PSW. In this regard, it is important that the PSW not assume child advocacy or investigative responsibilities directly, but remain focused on the needs of the non-offending parent.

Second, it is necessary to ameliorate the deleterious effects of institutional trauma, perpetrated by the intrusion of professionals into the life of the family. In the eyes of many investigative workers, a mother's ability to be emotionally supportive to her child reflects her ability to ensure the child's physical safety. Everson, Hunter, Runyon, Edelsohn, and Coulter (1989) found that when social service providers judge the mother to be unsupportive, the child is more likely to be placed outside the home, the child will more likely have to testify in court, and the child will display greater behavioural problems. They went on to warn that some mothers are caught in the dilemma of choosing between their adult male partner and their child. If a mother perceives she is blamed in some way for the assault, this may lead her to align with her more powerful male partner.

Dietz and Craft (1980) found that most social workers believe that mothers are as responsible for incest as the perpetrating fathers. The clinical literature on the subject of child sexual abuse has been ripe with mother-blaming (Elbow & Mayfield 1991). It seems that professionals have underplayed the devastating emotional turmoil that most parents experience after a disclosure of sexual abuse and the forces that push non-offending parents into confusion and disbelief (Everson et al. 1989; Byerly 1985). There are clinicians who eschew use of the term 'non-offending,' believing all parents must carry responsibility for creating the incest situation. Given this bias in the treatment literature, it is no wonder that practitioners in this field have held a cynical view of the mother's role in the intrafamilial sexual assault of a child.

While it is important to acknowledge that mothers should be held accountable, though not solely responsible, for family structure and transactional processes (Gelinas 1986), this does not mean they should be blamed or seen as being collusive in all instances of intrafamilial child sexual abuse. Clearly, any work that can be done to clarify the relationship between investigative agencies and non-offending parents, and that can help a mother feel more secure that she will receive fair treatment from investigators, will be of important benefit to the mother and ultimately to the sexually abused child.

5

Coordinating Family-Focused Treatment Services

Therapeutic issues, when providing treatment in situations of child sexual abuse, are complex and difficult to resolve. A range of treatment modalities is often required in these complex and serious circumstances (Furniss 1991; Sgroi 1982; Thorman 1983; Trepper & Barrett, 1986). Therapy is usually provided by several different therapists, for family members who have different degrees of involvement. Because of the complexity of the treatment process, this chapter will focus more narrowly on the treatment phase of community coordination and will highlight some of the key strategic decisions that are required in the provision of family focused treatment for incest.

The Therapy Process

As indicated in the previous chapter, a case manager was assigned to each case by the service coordinator to specifically coordinate treatment activities soon after an investigation of intrafamilial child sexual abuse began. The case manager was responsible for formulating a treatment plan in consultation with the CFS abuse investigator and the service coordinator. In creating this plan the case manager considered a number of key questions, including: the reaction of the non-offending parent and siblings, potential legal outcomes, the nature of the offense, and the relationship of the victim to the offender. From this information, the case manager would begin to form a tentative clinical hypothesis about the functional meaning of incest within the family system. This hypothesis would facilitate the development of an initial treatment plan for a comprehensive and sequential intervention with the family. Decisions as to which members of the family required individual, group, or dyadic therapy were made and referrals to appropriate therapists took place. The following example[1] describes how the process worked:

A nine-year-old girl, Anne, disclosed sexual abuse by her seventeen-year-old brother, Keith. The investigation indicated that Anne had been fondled on a frequent basis and there had been occasional vaginal penetration by Keith over a period of three years. Anne was able to describe the abuse in detail. Her brother acknowledged his guilt when confronted with the evidence. The mother was appalled to hear of the abuse and acted immediately to protect her daughter. She described her own history of intrafamilial sexual abuse and stated she had tried to raise her son 'in a way such that this would never happen again in her family.' She felt intense anger and feelings of betrayal.

The CFS investigative workers felt confident that the mother would be able to protect Anne. Both children were left in the home with the understanding that all family members would receive treatment. Charges were laid against Keith and he was directed, through a court order, to participate in treatment. A parent support worker was assigned to the mother and worked with her on a number of issues. These included constructing a safety plan to prevent further abuse, helping her deal with her guilt at not being able to protect Anne and her anger towards her son, building supportive friendships and extended family networks that would help her through the crisis, and dealing with community and extended family reaction to the abuse disclosure.

A case manager, assigned almost immediately after the disclosure, started working with Keith during the time the mother was seeing the parent support worker. In reviewing the needs of the family members, the case manager decided that both Keith and

---

[1] The investigative worker in this case was Kathryn Levine and the case manager, Bill Warren. Both received primary supervision from George MacDonald. The parent support worker was Tracy Fedoruk, with Barry Trute as primary supervisor. Anne's therapist was Norma Tessier, and Harry Nott co-facilitated the young offenders group with Bill Warren.

Anne were in need of individual and group therapy. He made a referral to a therapist for Anne and maintained close contact with the therapist throughout the course of the therapy. The case manager conducted individual therapy with Keith and also co-led a group for juvenile offenders in which Keith was involved. The focus of this therapy was on (1) encouraging Keith to develop a greater understanding of how his behaviour had affected his sister, and how important it was to assume full responsibility for the abuse; (2) obtaining a detailed sexual history and discussing the abuse episodes; and (3) providing appropriate education regarding healthy sexuality. The case manager monitoring Keith's progress felt he was prepared for an 'apology session'[2] with Anne when he was able to show significant empathy for her and understood which factors had led to the assault.

Meanwhile, Anne's therapist worked with her on many issues, such as alleviating the shame she felt regarding the abuse, suggesting ways for Anne to protect herself from future abuse, building a sense of power and assertiveness, and helping her understand healthy sexuality. A group therapy experience was helpful for Anne because it gave her an opportunity to share her experience with others and to realize she was not alone in suffering sexual assault in the family.

After the mother stopped seeing the parent support worker the case manager met with the mother on several occasions, continuing to work on the themes previously identified as significant to her role as a parent.

Because all members of the family were making progress in therapy, the case manager arranged for an apology session in which Keith apologized to Anne and his mother, assumed responsibility for the abuse, and pledged that it would not happen again. Dyadic and conjoint family meetings were then held, focusing on future relationships among family members, how to prevent recurrence of abuse, and building a stronger, healthier sibling relationship.

With this family the case planning and management system worked well. The case manager worked together with probation

---

[2] For more detail regarding the principles and practice implications of 'apology sessions,' see Madanes (1990) and Trepper (1986).

services and the parent support worker to design a treatment plan that would best meet the needs of each member of the family. Frequent contact between the case manager and other involved therapists insured that each was aware of the progress the other members of the family were making, and that the therapists were working with and not against each other. The case manager was required to maintain contact with the therapist on a regular basis in order to evaluate the progress of each family member. Such contacts also provided an opportunity for the therapists to work as a team, brainstorm, set strategy, and provide peer supervision. Depending on the information gathered in these consultation meetings, a case manager might abandon an hypothesis, adjust it, or develop whole new interventions to test a new hypothesis. The information provided in these meetings served as a basis for decisions regarding the ongoing course of therapy.

In some cases, especially with 'resistant' families, struggles arose between the child protection agency and the case manager regarding what treatment was in the best interests of the child. This became a concern primarily when the children had been apprehended, and when treatment providers disagreed as to the advisability of returning them home. In these cases, it became clear that the statutory agency needed to establish both control and limit-setting at the initiation of treatment. Woodard and Woodard (1983) have been critical of child protection agencies who break up families ostensibly to protect children, but who do not provide definitions of what 'successful therapy' would look like. They suggest:

> Any contract for family therapy should be more clearly stated ...
> The therapist, must negotiate job descriptions (of a sort) so that who's responsible for what is clear. The agency must be encouraged to state specifically the kinds of changes that are expected so that later decisions are not left to the whims or feelings of the case worker involved. Negotiating clear goals for treatment from the agency is identical and as difficult as negotiating with the family (p. 33).

In a similar manner, Sgroi (1982) states that it is of the utmost importance to formulate a treatment plan for incestuous families that is specific with regard to behavioral expectations. She states that the family's problems must be defined as clearly as possible and that treatment monitoring and intervention should always be done in the overall context of the treatment plan and include clinical indicators of behavioural change.

The following goals for change were created by child protection staff participating in the coordinated community service system. These were to serve as examples of items that could be tailored to family circumstances in which father – daughter incest was the presenting problem and in which family reconstitution was the goal. Again, we should state that treatment contracts and specific indicators of behavioural change will vary according to situational or contextual differences in families. We should also state that changes in the legal status of children should not be solely dependent on the completion of all aspects of treatment or the achievement of all the goals contained in a treatment contract. Negotiations between the protection agency, the clients, and the clients' therapists should always be welcomed as long as the spirit and intent of the contract is respected.

The following are some specific factors that indicate when treatment had been successful, and when important changes have occurred in a family with father–daughter incest:

The Perpetrator

1. Perpetrators give full disclosure and acknowledgment of responsibility. (This is a fundamental requirement.) Rehabilitated perpetrators in therapy come to be brutally honest about their sexual transgressions and can talk about their past without embarrassment. In fact, they will often reveal sexual offenses in excess of what their victim disclosed (Ellis 1990).

2. Where therapy is successful, perpetrators are very aware of the impact their assaults have had on the child victims and they can talk about what it means for the children now and in their future life. They understand the critical importance of taking full responsibility for their actions and not blaming the victims for the sexual abuse. As part of this acceptance of responsibility, they recognize that their behaviour has broken a bond of trust and seriously undermined their role as fathers.

3.   Perpetrators show awareness of societal influences on how sexuality and power are expressed and they are cognizant of the exploitive and deleterious effects of pornography.

4.   ، Perpetrators can talk about experiences of their own childhood or early adolescent sexual socialization that conditioned them to sexually offend against their own children. This includes a basic understanding of their family of origin with respect to healthy and unhealthy family sexuality, the influence of gender on individual behaviour, role modelling of gender, role modelling of fatherly and motherly roles, how their family fits within their social and cultural community. All are important aspects of what perpetrators must understand. They will be able to 'surface,' or bring to consciousness, episodes of abuse and repressed pain regarding their experiences of victimization and perpetration.

5.   The perpetrator understands his wife and is aware of key themes in her own family experience. He is able to talk with her about her parents and their modelling of father – mother roles. He can speak with her about any similar experiences she may have had in her family of origin and what it has meant to her. He can speak with her about unresolved issues she may have with her parents and siblings. He can help her talk about issues she may be hesitant to talk about.

6.   The perpetrator understands the complex familial stresses that have contributed to his offending pattern in his family of procreation. He also understands his relationship with his wife and the problems in their marital relationship. He comes to understand how his family of origin has influenced him and how these historical patterns come into play in his family of procreation. He understands how his past life experience set the stage for the abandonment of his role as a father. He also comes to understand the relationship between himself and his abused and non-abused children. He understands the relationship between the non-offending parent and the victim and non-victims.

7. The perpetrator understands his sexual offending pattern and recognizes the cues that start the pattern. Through treatment, and his own emerging thoughtfulness, the perpetrator has a plan developed to block the offending pattern and he implements such a plan upon recognition of the cues.

The Non-Offending Parent

1. The non-offending parent accepts the victim's allegations, and desires to protect the child – two prerequisites to further treatment. The mother does not hold the victim accountable for the molestation (Server 1982) but directs appropriate emotion and accountability toward the perpetrator. The non-offending parent is willing to hear all the details of the victimization and its frequency and duration. She needs to be able to confront the father, to disagree with him, to act despite his objections, and to intercede on behalf of the children (Faller 1988). She is motivated not only to protect her children but to work towards change in the family that will ensure their safety and protection.

2. The non-offending parent is keenly aware of the impact the assaults have had on the victim and can talk about what it may mean for the child now and in her future life. She understands the importance of supporting the child as an innocent victim and recognizes her own possible failures in her parenting duties. She deals openly with her own feelings of guilt and betrayal regarding the sexual abuse.

3. The non-offending parent is aware of key elements in her husband's own childhood and the early experiences that have contributed to his behaviour. She is able to talk with him about his parents and their modelling of father – mother roles. She has an understanding of his family of origin's view of human sexuality and gender roles. The non-offending parent encourages her partner's exploration and expression of the repressed details of his own victimization, as well as his perpetration of sexual abuse. She can pursue a discussion of these matters even when her partner finds it difficult to talk about them.

4. The non-offending parent has a clear understanding of her own family of origin. She understands what her parents and the wider community milieux taught her about family sexuality and the influence of gender on individual behaviour. This includes an awareness of the differences in the modelling of mother and father roles and how her family dynamics fit into larger social and cultural expectations. She is able to talk about any experiences she may have had as a victim and how these experiences influenced her life.

5. The non-offending parent understands the complex familial stresses that play a part in the creation of the incest dynamic. This understanding includes struggling with current marital problems, sexual or otherwise. She accepts the notion that her family of origin makes up the better part of herself and that this 'self' formed a 'fit' with her offending partner. She is able to talk about experiences of victimization that may have inhibited her functioning as a wife and mother. She is able to understand her relationship with the victim and any of her children who were not direct victims of abuse. She understands the relationships between the offender and his victim, and between the offender and the children he did not victimize directly.

6. The non-offending parent understands her husband's explanation of his offending pattern and recognizes the cues that start the pattern. Through treatment and in dialogue with her partner the non-offending spouse understands what part, if any, she can play in helping her husband overcome his inappropriate sexual predilections.

The Victim

1. The victim has progressed through therapy to a point where she has abandoned all feelings of responsibility for the abuse. (This responsibility varies according to the cognitive and developmental stages of the child. For example, school-age children are less likely than preschoolers to internalize feelings of responsibility for the perpetrator's actions. At the same time,

preschoolers continue to express a strong affective investment in both parents.) In cases where the incest has caused family breakup through the loss of one or more of its members, the victim understands that the breakup was precipitated by the actions of the parent and through no fault of her own. The child has learned through therapy that the eventual reunification of the family will be decided by the mandated agency.

2. Where therapy is successful, the victim can articulate the consequences of the sexual abuse on herself as a person. Friedrich (1990) suggests that there will be a range in the degree of trauma the victim experiences. Many children understand at some level, commensurate with their age, the loss of their childhood through sexual exploitation. The victim can express her sense of betrayal, powerlessness, and loss of faith in her parents. Many children experience generic behavioural disorders as a consequence of having been sexually abused within their families. These behaviours, running from mild to serious, include pseudo-maturity, self-injurious or otherwise destructive behaviours, psychosomatic problems, psycho-sexual disorders, and clinical depression. The victim, through successful therapy, will be helped to recognize that these behaviours stem directly from the incestuous contact and are not derived solely from her own intra-psychic pathology or 'personal craziness.'

3. When developmentally appropriate, the victim can articulate the differences between her family and a family where sexual abuse would not occur. She understands the differences between healthy and unhealthy family sexuality, appropriate and inappropriate mother/father roles, and gender differences.

4. When the victim remains in the family, she has a well developed safety plan. This plan includes how she will relate to the offender and what she will do if the offender initiates a sexual contact. The plan also includes a trusted adult that she will immediately disclose to at the first sign of untoward sexual behaviour on the part of the offender. Future family therapy sessions can deal with the implications of such a plan for the whole family, especially as it impacts upon restoration of the parental hierarchy and more normal family functioning.

Non-Victimized Children in the Family

Siblings of the victim who have not apparently been abused have been referred to as undetected victims (Cohen 1983). With respect to abusive patterning in a family, non-victimized siblings of a victim must be an important focus in any therapeutic intervention, as the following factors indicate.

1. Siblings of victimized children within incestuous families typically align with the parental dyad upon disclosure and project the blame and responsibility for disrupting the family on to the victim. With successful treatment, siblings acknowledge that incest has occurred within the family and understand that the responsibility for it lies with the offender.

2. Siblings express empathy and support for the victim. In addition, they acknowledge their conflicting loyalties. They express their own sense of confusion, sadness, and betrayal, but not in the guise of blaming the victim.

3. Siblings understand the family patterns that contributed to the incest. Appropriate to their age, they recognize differences in gender roles, power differentials, and hierarchies. They also understand when such structural aspects of their family are not satisfactory.

4. Siblings need to have open discussion of and a resolution to the feelings of jealousy, resentment, and exclusion that often occur in incestuous families. For instance, they need to acknowledge feelings such as anger at not having been the favoured child. On the other hand, some siblings may have felt tremendous fear that they were potential victims and, as a result, unconsciously colluded with the offender.

Dealing with individual experiences of siblings is important because it is issues such as these, remaining unresolved, which may set the stage for the transmission of incest to succeeding generations.

In their recent report of indicators that professionals apply to decisions regarding family reunification after treatment for incest, Kinder Matthews, Raymaker, and Speltz (1991) identify a set of behavioural preconditions that correspond closely to those we have identified as appropriate to expect from perpetrators, non-offending parents, victims, and other children in the family. They add an additional set of preconditions for family reunification (over and above the adequate completion of family therapy) that relate to the family system as a whole. These include the ability to discuss the sexual abuse openly and together, an understanding of potentially risky situations and family protection plans, and family involvement in a social support system that prevents social isolation (p. 149).

In the coordinated treatment system the drafting of a 'treatment contract' became a routine procedure with families that were resistant to initiating therapy. Such a contract was also found to be useful in situations that involved child apprehension or had the potential to require child apprehension. The primary purpose of these formal treatment contracts (which required parent signatures to acknowledge understanding of and agreement with the terms) was to maintain clarity as to what behaviours the child welfare agency needed to observe to know that a child's safety could be protected. These treatment contracts identified specific therapeutic goals concerned with the prevention of further abuse and the restoration of stable family functioning. In addition, they described in some detail what a family needed to learn before it could begin to accept responsibility for its own satisfactory functioning without long-term dependence on supporting agencies. Within the parameters of these contracts parents were free to chose their own therapists or could elect to have the agency secure therapists for them. The contracts were helpful also in a number of other ways. They were specific as to what needed to happen next, and what clients could do to regain their independence from professional intrusion.

It became clear over time in our project that it was the responsibility of the child protection personnel not only to suggest what elements of treatment were required but also to provide clear guidance concerning what needed to change before they felt it was safe to return apprehended children. To this end, investigative workers began to identify detailed indicators of change suitable for each particular family. They would then convene meetings with family members and their therapists to specify areas of treatment they felt needed to be addressed.

This whole process established the protection agency as ultimately responsible for the safety and protection of the children in the family. It established therapists outside the protection agency as responsible for therapy and for providing, to the utmost of their ability, a means for the client to achieve the goals defined by the agency.

By establishing itself as the 'control agent' at the outset of the family's involvement with the investigation team, the child protection agency acted as a lightening rod for clients' anger at being locked into therapy, thereby allowing the assigned case manager and the therapists to be in a much more neutral relationship with the client. Those providing therapy could then work effectively with family members to help them achieve the personal growth necessary to have their children returned and get the child protection staff 'off their backs.'

The creation of a safety plan for incestuous families is a notion derived from the 'addictions model' of sexually abusive families. It is a procedure that should be instituted when a child is left in a home with an alleged perpetrator or when a protection agency contemplates returning children before all family therapy is completed. As such, the plan must be on the agenda of a therapist for continuous monitoring, since leaving it in place automatically precludes the possibility of fully restoring the parental hierarchy. That is to say, if the father must always guard against an impulse 'beyond' his control, if the child must always be on her guard against the father's 'impulses' and the mother always vigilant and closely protective, does this leave a place for a 'responsible father' within the family?

Establishment of clear issues of control and limit-setting for family members does a number of things of importance in the handling of child abuse cases. When the child protection agency establishes clear expectations at the beginning of the investigation, it establishes appropriate boundaries between itself and the family, and between itself and other helping agencies or treatment teams, which in turn contribute to overall boundary clarification. Boundary diffusion between the roles of parents and child welfare workers in situations of child abuse can contribute significantly to ongoing family dysfunction. Boundary diffusion within a multiagency system of service delivery can also contribute to further deterioration within the abusive family (Dale Davies 1985).

A distinction can be made between three different types of basic services provided in situations of child sexual abuse (Furniss 1991). Each is based on a different mandate in service delivery, is driven by a different set of service objectives, and is framed by a different basic ideology of practice. The 'Primary Punitive Intervention' is focused on punishment of the abuser and seeks to deter unlawful acts. The 'Primary Child Protective Intervention' is focused primarily on protecting the mental and physical well-being of children and encouraging their positive moral and social development. The 'Primary Therapeutic Intervention' is focused on the amelioration of psychological distress in all individuals with trauma associated with child sexual abuse. It recognizes the fundamental importance of intervening in the family system in order to alter dynamics and relationships and achieve long-term and positive resolution of the toxic effects of child sexual abuse.

These differing perspectives on the delivery of services cannot be directly blended or easily integrated. Perhaps the key to integrating each of these necessary service sectors is to heighten interprofessional awareness of the need for each and the importance each can play in responding to this serious societal issue. Awareness of roles and respect for the value of allied service sectors may serve to open the paths to collaborative and integrated action.

Even when there is a recognition of the importance of both child protection and therapeutic services, there will be disputes over the degree to which each service sector should exercise control over a case. During the course of the project, a problem often emerged subsequent to the completion of a treatment contract. As cases were assigned by the service coordinator to specific case managers with professional positions outside the child protection agency, it became clear that some therapists were unsure as to what constituted adequate change in specific types of behaviour within a sexually abusive family relative to the specific goals within the treatment contract. In essence, disagreement arose over who was controlling the therapeutic aspects of the case. Not only did there need to be detailed behavioural indicators of whether treatments were successful, but also there had to be an understanding of who would determine how the objectives would be reached or what treatment procedures should be employed. Some case managers argued that while a case had been assigned to them, the protection agency never really gave up control, including their wish to oversee the process of the therapy.

The force and power of triangulation in agency relations is well recognized in the family therapy literature (Carl & Jurkovic 1983; Imber-Black 1991). Agency triangulation occurs when a family forms conflicting alliances with several different human service agencies. For example, parents in a family in which incest has occurred may closely align with a family therapist at a community mental health centre and attempt to develop an alliance with this therapist against a child and family service agency. The family then elicits support from the mental health worker to help them deal with the expectations of the child protection plan. Consider the following example.[3]

A disclosure of father-daughter incest was made to CFS by an uncle of the daughter. Subsequent medical examination confirmed that there had been vaginal penetration of the young girl. The father acknowledged the abuse and both parents agreed to treatment. Despite this compliance, the agency decided that a one-year temporary order of guardianship was necessary. They did not feel the mother was in a position to protect her child. In a contested court hearing the agency was granted this order. Over the year the parents agreed voluntarily to see two therapists from a local mental health unit while the daughter attended individual and group therapy.

Problems among the workers arose during the year. The parents' therapists believed the parents had made progress and should have their child returned to them, while the child's therapist felt she was not ready to return home. CFS, in reviewing the situation, felt the parents had made too few changes and it decided to go for another temporary order. This difference of opinion created a great deal of conflict and distrust among the various therapists and the CFS. After much discussion, a plan of action evolved that was agreeable to all parties. Expectations that the parents had to meet before the child returned home were clearly identified and understood by all parties involved, including the members of the family.

To be effective the therapist must seek open and functional alliances with both the family and other larger systems such as the child welfare agency. This is particularly important for the practitioner

---

[3] The child protection worker in this case was Harry Nott with primary supervision from George MacDonald. The family therapist was Kurt Guenther. Individual therapists were Kathy Genoway, Kurt Guenther, and Ron Laverty. The group therapist was Audrey Armstrong with supervision from Liz Adkins.

who is responsible for the family's treatment. It requires a clinical stance that frees family therapists from their desire to protect the family and be its confidante, while simultaneously leaving them free of the powerful pull of professional alliances (Imber Coopersmith 1982).

In another situation that exemplified agency triangulation, a mother attempted to initiate child protection services against her husband through the staff of a women's shelter to which she and her children had been recently admitted. In essence, she attempted to have the shelter join with her in pursuing a child welfare intervention into the life of the family.

A worker from a local family violence shelter phoned CFS requesting service for a mother and her two children. The CFS worker, having had contact with the mother in prior abuse allegations against her husband, stated that she would not intervene if the mother did not disclose the circumstances of the abuse. Soon after, the shelter worker phoned stating that the mother had disclosed that her husband had physically and sexually abused the children. Because of a history of lack of trust between the shelter and the CFS agency, the CFS worker had misgivings about this disclosure, questioning whether the mother had been prodded in order to obtain help from CFS. This distrust was heightened when the mother reneged on her disclosure in interviews with the police and the CFS worker's investigation was not as thorough as the shelter staff member would have liked. At the beginning of the meeting there was evident tension between the two workers. The heated verbal exchange included accusations of lying, withholding evidence, supporting offenders, and victimizing abused women. With the help of mediation by members of the community treatment committee, both workers were able to express their feelings frankly to each other, opening the door for examination of the real issues in the case.

When interprofessional disagreements arise, open discussion is essential for their resolution. Respectful and candid communication needs to be maintained to resolve differences and avoid the blaming and mistrust that is all too common between professionals in child sexual abuse cases.

A variation of agency triangulation is interagency hostility based on 'conflict by proxy' (Furniss 1991). In this situation, hostilities and conflicts within the family unit are played out by different agencies, in separate alliances with different members of the family. These might involve coalitions of the victim and her or his therapist against the non-offending parent(s) and his or her therapist, or against the offender and his or her therapist. The struggles that ensue in such coalitions do not help the victim and his or her family (Woodard & Woodard, 1983). As Imber Coppersmith (1982) comments:

> The boundaries between a family and larger systems may be too diffuse, handicapping the family's own coping resources; or too rigid, preventing the utilization of needed assistance. When family–agency boundaries are diffuse, frequently the agency will define the family's problems for it, become entangled in aspects of the family's life that are not the purview of the particular agency, and alternate between overprotecting family members and becoming exasperated with them (p. 5).

The importance of maintaining clear boundaries between the roles and responsibilities of family members and the various service agencies involved is paramount.

Another fundamental challenge facing case managers and clinical practitioners, particularly from the non-mandated agencies (i.e., not child welfare or probation services), is to understand adequately the inherent differences in therapy when working with 'involuntary' versus 'voluntary' families. Prior to their commitment to work with project cases, most community professionals had generally been involved with families that utilized their services on a voluntary basis. When these agencies worked with involuntary families they experienced them as complicated, demanding, and requiring the use of different therapeutic skills and attitudes. In this sense, much new learning was required.

The key to this issue is the need for clarity regarding the nature of the therapeutic relationship and the belief by many therapists that the healing process can not be framed by coercion of any kind, but must be fundamentally based on a relationship of trust and confidence. The identification of child sexual abuse as an 'addictive disorder' (Furniss 1991) establishes a meaningful therapeutic metaphor. Although the somatic effects of withdrawal are not present, as they are in chemical addiction, similar elements of compulsive behaviour (e.g., secrecy and uncontrolled urges) are present.

It is our belief that some coercive aspects, such as court-mandated therapy or confrontation in group settings, are often essential treatment prerequisites to insight-based therapies. Protective actions and attempts to exercise control can be done by the courts. Court action is in fact vital in many incest cases to bring family members to therapy and to keep them there. In this sense it is important for child welfare staff to base their decisions regarding child protection actions on the agreement by the family to engage in treatment and the agreement of parents to secure safety in the home. As Furniss (1991) points out, 'Without child protective action the child will be both without therapy and without protection from further abuse' (p. 97).

Another frequently discussed issue for therapists working with the family as a system, or with individual family members, was the struggle to remain neutral and non-blaming as called for in a family systems approach to therapy.

We are not suggesting here that the therapist or worker should always be absolutely neutral. It is essential that a victim receive help from someone who clearly believes and supports him or her. It is important that the perpetrator know and accept that he is held responsible for his sexual assault on his child. Similarly, it is important that non-offending parents feel the therapist is on their side and is not intent on punishing them for the abuse their children have suffered. However, it is clear that distorted alliances between a professional and a family member (or subsystem) can cause grief both within and outside the family.

Furniss (1991) offers valuable insights in this regard when he differentiates between punitive or confrontational 'linear' interventions – those required in assigning responsibility for illegal and socially inappropriate behaviour such as incest – and 'systemic' interventions – those that seek to alter patterns of human interaction and restructure the family as a social entity. Even when responsibility was clearly established for abusive behaviour and there was sexual safety in the family, some therapists sometimes ran the risk of losing their therapeutic neutrality, and would feel compelled to join with children against one or both parents. A therapist working with a child victim may be drawn quickly to side with the child against the parents, thereby losing sight of the family as a whole. It does happen as well, in some situations in which incest has occurred, that a therapist working with the parents may align too closely with the idea of 'saving the family,' and may lose sight of the needs of the victim. These distorted alliances were usually spotted by another professional working with the family or its members. The alliances then became the focal point of interagency conflict in the coordinated service system. It was the case manager's responsibility, in consultation with the service coordinator, to be aware of these dangers and to work towards resolving any such problems that arose during the course of therapy.

Coordinated Services: A Case Study

The following case study[4] describes the progress of one family through the various stages of the coordinated community service model, including the sequential manner in which treatment services were initiated and maintained:

The F Family

Mr and Mrs F and their family of four children live in a small town in rural Manitoba. The children are Marcel, 20, Alain, 19, Denise, 15, and Angel, 13.

A local school principal called the child and family service agency to report that Denise had contacted him saying she was afraid to go home and that she had not been home for the past week. Denise reported that her younger sister Angel had gone to the RCMP the week before and disclosed that she had been sexually assaulted by her older brother, Marcel. Angel had subsequently been told to leave the house by her parents and was staying with a cousin in a nearby city. The project service coordinator was informed and the case was assigned to a child welfare abuse investigator.

---

[4] The child protection worker in this case was Debbie Shannon and the case manager was Bill Warren with primary supervision to both provided by George MacDonald. The parent support worker was Mary Anne Hildebrand. Individual treatment was provided by Bill Warren and Audrey Armstrong.

The investigation

When the school principal informed the CFS intake worker that the youngest daughter had already made a statement to police, it was clear that the police had failed to report to the child protection agency (as should be done through the Manitoba Guidelines 'Child Abuse Enforcement'). A telephone call to the responsible police detachment confirmed that this young woman had made a statement to the police the previous week and that they had meant to contact the child protection agency. The CFS child abuse investigator reiterated the policy guidelines and indicated that the police's failure to communicate with the CFS meant that no agency was looking after the safety and protection of the two young women in the F family. The RCMP indicated they were aware that Angel had been asked to leave the family home but felt she was capable of arranging her own living arrangements.

During this conversation, the police officer informed the child-welfare abuse investigator that the police had not yet interviewed the oldest daughter, Denise. Arrangements were made immediately to do the interview jointly with the police and the child protection agency. The child-welfare abuse investigator, in consultation with her supervisor, made a decision at that time to apprehend both girls. The parents were informed of the CFS agency decision and the father complained that the two girls were trying to 'make trouble for the family.' Both parents felt that the two girls were better off in a foster home since they were 'troublemakers.'

The joint interview with Denise confirmed her sister's earlier disclosure to the police that their twenty-year-old brother had been sexually assaulting them both for the past three years. Specifically, he would come into the girls' bedroom during the night and fondle their breast and vaginal areas. At one time he had digitally penetrated his youngest sister.

Both Denise and Angel informed the child abuse investigator that they did not feel comfortable at home because the parents would not allow them to have a door on their bedroom. In addition, both thought their mother greatly favoured their brothers and was emotionally abusive towards her daughters. She had told them she 'wished they had never been born.'

The child abuse investigator in collaboration with the police set up a number of interviews to confirm the information given by the two girls. An appointment was arranged for both girls to be medically examined. Their medical exam was consistent with their disclosures.

Separate interviews with Marcel were conducted by the police and the child protection agency. In both interviews, Marcel acknowledged he had committed the offenses described by his sisters. When the parents were informed of the allegations and their son's admission of guilt, the mother became extremely critical of her daughters, suggesting that the sexual assaults had probably been orchestrated in part by the girls themselves (by their manner of dress and by leading their brother on).

Problems in the disclosure phase

There was a problem with this particular police detachment, who were not following provincial policy guidelines on reporting child abuse. Because they had already interviewed one of the victims, it was necessary that she be interviewed a second time by a child and family services investigator. The way the police handled the case also suggested they did not understand that determining the safety of children was a jurisdictional matter for the CFS agency. Their decision to take the one girl's statement and allow her to return home made both girls vulnerable to family retribution. It also suggested they did not take the assaults on the girls seriously.

This police detachment was actually outside the research project area. Because of this, they were not sufficiently familiar with the procedural protocals endorsed by the sub-division inspector or with the project's goal to increase service coordination. At the time this case came into the project, the service coordinator made an appointment with the detachment sergeant to reiterate the coordinator's concerns about the handling of the case. The sergeant explained that the case had been mishandled because of new members of the police force who did not understand provincial policy. Problems with this detachment did not recur on any other case.

In view of the parents' refusal to support the daughters, the girls were initially apprehended by the CFS agency. Neither the police nor the parents were willing to have the perpetrator removed from the home. Both Mr and Mrs F minimized the sexual assaults on their daughters and claimed they were troublemakers. Both agreed that their daughters live in foster homes until they could deal with the crisis. In interviewing family members, the CFS investigative worker was not assured that the parents would protect the girls from further abuse.

After the initial apprehension the CFS worker continued her assessment of the family to determine how the protection agency should proceed. She concluded that, although the parents were at first angry with their daughters because of the family crisis brought on by their disclosure, they did love their daughters and were willing to engage in treatment. After some involvement with the CFS worker, the parents agreed to sign a 'voluntary placement agreement' for six months with the goal of stopping the abuse, considering the family situation, and working towards having the girls return home.

The worker utilized a number of approaches in treating the family. She connected with them in a supportive manner, refusing to get caught in an adversarial 'us versus them' approach. She focused on the love the parents had for their children, rather than on their apparent rejection of their daughters. Most important, perhaps, she respected their beliefs about religion and family functioning. For example, upon being offered the services of the parent support worker and a case manager by the CFS child abuse investigator, the couple initially refused, insisting that they were Catholic and could only be seen by a Christian counsellor. Through the use of biblical metaphor (Parents are like the good shepherds who, in losing one sheep from their fold, will leave the ninety-nine to go and search for the one that is lost.), the worker facilitated a stronger sense of commitment in the parents. The child abuse investigator was able to convince the parents that they could be more supportive to their daughters, and that the counselling they would receive would be consistent with their own beliefs. A parent support worker (who shared the same religious beliefs as the family) was assigned to the case by the service coordinator and she continued the work with Mr and Mrs F.

In the judgment of both the CFS child abuse investigator and the parent support worker, there was enough positive feeling developing between the F. family and the CFS agency that the assignment of a CFS case manager could be achieved without fear on the part of the parents. The transition between the PSW and the assigned case manager occurred smoothly and comfortably for the family. The ease with which these transitions were made seemed directly attributable to the confidence and trust inspired by both the child abuse investigator and parent support worker. Because of the availability on the part of the whole family and its willingness to change, the child abuse investigator did not feel it necessary to formalize a treatment contract with this family. However, care was taken to ensure that the goals for therapy were clear.

The assigned case manager continued to engage the F family in a manner that was sensitive to their needs. In the initial stages of therapy, he explained in precise detail how he saw the progress of therapy and what tasks they would have to deal with over time. He provided some tentative forecasting of the approximate amount of time therapy would take (thereby helping the family to see that there would be an end to it in reasonable time and that the identified goals were achievable). He explained that he was responsible in an overall sense for all of the therapy, but that he would ask other therapists to take responsibility for certain specialized parts of it (e.g., a female therapist for the two female victims). He explained to the parents that the ultimate goal – the return of their two daughters – would be decided eventually by them and the CFS abuse investigator when he was able to report to CFS that everyone in the family had made sufficient progress to warrant such a move.

The case manager for the family performed this role in the ideal sense. He was able to function in a positive and neutral manner (being equally available to meet the needs of each of its members). By calling frequent meetings with other professionals involved in the treatment, he was able to gauge progress of treatment as both individuals and family moved through the respective stages of therapy.

The case manager formulated a tentative clinical hypothesis about the F family in the early stages of his involvement with them. The parents informed him that the two girls had been showing behavioural problems for some time before their disclosure to the police. They saw Marcel as a 'different boy' who had few friends and seemed distant from his siblings. The parents seemed to be a traditional Christian couple who supported a rigid patriarchal system where men were 'rightfully in charge of the family.' Mrs F was inclined to support this position by minimizing the actions of Marcel and blaming her daughters for being provocative.

Early on in the treatment process, the case manager speculated that Mrs F had been an incest victim herself and that she dealt with it by attributing blame to herself and repressing memory of the abuse. Based on the available information, the case manager hypothesized that the 'acting out' behaviour of the girls was directly attributable to the sexual assaults of the brother. At a broader level, he also questioned the inherent sexism of the family. To Marcel, by his own admission, the incest was a way of stopping his parent's tendency to ignore him and favour his brother, and to seek affection from his more vulnerable sisters. The incest itself was consistent with the worst aspects of a family system overly dominated by gender inequality. The case manager set out to help the family restructure itself in a number of specific ways, by providing

1. individual and group therapy for the victims, which encouraged the young women to continue to build their self-esteem and sense of power and to recognize their right to be treated with respect;

2. individual therapy for the perpetrator, in which he was able to explore the rationale for his assaults and find a meaning within the context of his family. In so doing, the offender was able to confront his parents in a productive way while expressing genuine remorse to his two sisters.

3. marital sessions for the parents, which enabled both to look at their family in a more objective fashion and acknowledge the apparent inequalities with which they treated their children. Encouraging these parents to begin supporting their daughters not only helped them acknowledge the ways in which they had betrayed their daughter's trust, it helped them to see how all the children had suffered in different ways. Mrs. F. began to explore her own family background, which helped her see her family of procreation from a new perspective. She and her husband also received help to redefine their marital life together.

4. male sub-system sessions that, helped all the men to see that males can take responsibility for their inappropriate behaviours, show remorse, and even cry, and in so doing can discover a new-found respect for themselves. In the case of Marcel, he began to relate to his brother in a new and respectful manner.

5.   reconstitutive family therapy, which allowed all family members to acknowledge how they felt with one another in complementary ways, and to challenge some of their previously destructive ways of being together. These sessions allowed the offender and the parents to apologize and to forgive so that the family experienced a genuine reconstruction of their lives together.

Problems in the treatment stage

Only one major service problem surfaced with the F family during the course of their treatment. It became evident at the time of Marcel's court sentencing. When the judge ordered Marcel to enter a period of supervised probation, a probation officer (a project participant) and the family's local pastor took it upon themselves to find a residential treatment program for him without consulting the case manager. This of course was not part of the coordinated treatment plan, and it briefly confused both perpetrator and family as to who was in charge of their case. The case manager contacted the probation officer and the priest, reviewed the goals of the project, and was able to resolve the issue quickly.

The daughters in the F family, Denise and Angel, were returned to the family home a short time after the expiration of the agency's temporary order. Both have returned to high school and are doing well. Marcel has left home, secured employment, and is now living independently. Mr and Mrs F still struggle with the changes in their relationship resulting from the therapy, but their struggle now seems a much healthier one.

The F family progressed through the Rural Child Sexual Abuse Project in the most optimal way. Coordination from the time of disclosure up to the last family session was well planned and sequential. At each step along the path, the family was made aware of what would happen next, thereby decreasing their anxiety and the potential for interagency service fragmentation. Much of the success in this case can be attributed to a group of professionals, who not only understood the importance of systemic work with families, but who also maintained clear and precise professional boundaries. In essence, everyone understood what everyone else's job was, and little time was spent in unproductive interagency struggles.

Systemic Treatment Services with a Single Therapist

Not all child sexual abuse cases require the involvement of a team of treatment providers. As a minimum we found that one person with a child protection role and one with a family therapist role was required. In some instances a case manager elected to assume all therapeutic responsibilities and, with the concurrence of the service coordinator, created a treatment plan within which the case manager was the only therapist involved with all members of the family. On the infrequent occasions that this could be done, a smoother sequential treatment process could be implemented. It did, however, require a considerable investment of time by the sole family therapist. Single therapist treatment situations were most often those involving voluntary clients within affection-based sexual abuse circumstances (see Larson & Maddock 1986). The following is an example of one such case.[5]

The D Family

Mr and Mrs D lived with their five children in a small town. The parents were forty and thirty-six years old respectively. They were a professional couple who in the past number of years had often moved from town to town as the father was promoted. The family had lived in this town for about eight months. With each successive promotion, the parents recognized that the father was becoming more and more absent from the family as he kept up to the demands of each new workplace. Mrs D had very recently returned to part-time employment outside the home. The five children in the family included Brian, 12, Fred, 11, Lisa, 10, and Judy and David, 6-year-old twins.

Mr and Mrs D contacted Child and Family Services because of a disclosure by ten-year-old Lisa involving her brother Brian. A friend of Mrs D's advised her to call because she knew CFS dealt with child sexual abuse cases. Mrs D told the agency that her daughter had disclosed that on several occasions 'she had taken her clothes off and her brother had been on top of her.' She indicated that at one time he had attempted intercourse, but 'it hurt and she

---

[5] Diane deLucia was case manager, with primary supervision provided by George MacDonald.

cried and he stopped.' The daughter, at the time of the disclosure, expressed shame and guilt for something that had apparently gone on for approximately two years. She was worried also that if her father were told she might lose his love.

At the time of the disclosure, the mother indicated that she was shocked and angry with her son. Although she was fearful of her husband's reaction she did inform him of what happened and found him to be supportive in dealing with both children. Each of the parents were shocked, angry, and disappointed with their son but were able to separate his incestuous behaviour from his other positive attributes.

Disclosure and investigation

Because the perpetrator in the D family was twelve years old at the time of disclosure, his actions could not be considered sexual abuse under the Child and Family Services Act (i.e., he was not considered to have the care, custody, or control of his younger siblings). In addition, because the parents made a voluntary disclosure to the protection agency and were seeking counselling, the service coordinator referred the family to a case manager who became involved with them immediately. The case manager consulted the police to confirm that Brian's involvement with his sister could not be regarded as a criminal act because of their ages. The police concurred.

Prior to the development of a specific treatment plan, the case manager explored the allegations further with the children. It was learned that prior to the disclosure, when Brian and Lisa were ten and eight, they periodically would play 'doctor,' undress, and examine each other. At first this would occur during playtime. Eventually, it would occur when Brian was babysitting his sisters and brother. They would also tie each other up while pretending, each in their turn, to be hostage and kidnapper. This would always occur with sex play. As the game became progressively more sexual, Lisa began to feel more and more uncomfortable. She decided to tell her mother because she was feeling shame and guilt. When she disclosed, her brother was extremely angry with her because he believed she played an equal part in the sexual activity.

During the initial stages of treatment, the case manager lent an educational videotape (regarding the creation of sexual safety in the

family and community) to this family to view. The parents were
also given information regarding its potential use in their family.
Soon after, the youngest boy disclosed that he too had been molested by his older brother. These incidents occurred during show-
ers at bedtime. The older brother would rub his penis on the
younger boy's 'bum' and genital area. He would ask his younger
brother to do the same to him but the younger brother refused. At
the time of disclosure, Brian believed his brother liked this sexual
touching and he did not believe coercion was in any way involved.
The case manager recognized that these beliefs, and the young offender's perceptions about compliance in sexual play by his sister
and brother, would be major issues in treatment.

One further disclosure of sexual abuse was made by the mother
in this family. When she was twelve years old, she had been sexually molested by her father. At that time, he had fondled her breasts
and attempted to touch her genital area. She immediately told him
to stop or she would tell her mother. He did stop and never made a
second attempt. She told no one of this incident, except her husband when they were engaged to be married. She disclosed it to the
case manager for two reasons. First, the shame and guilt about her
early experience with her father was renewed by this incident with
her eldest son. Second, she wanted to help her daughter and
younger son deal with their emotional response to the sexual abuse
by articulating any painful feelings they might have (and which she
remembered holding inside herself as a child).

Child and Family Services were satisfied that the parents were
taking immediate steps to alter their supervisory patterns with respect to all of the children, including removing Brian from all child-
care responsibility. Because of the openness of this family and their
availability to treatment there were no service difficulties in the
disclosure phase of services. The family was considered ideal for
immediate referral to a case manager and allied providers of
treatment.

The treatment process

As soon as they had discovered the incestuous activity of their oldest son, the parents had contacted the CFS agency for help in dealing with the problem. Because the family was voluntary and a systemic treatment plan could be quickly implemented by the case

manager, a parent support worker was not assigned. The case manager did, however, perceive that some crisis intervention was immediately needed by the parents and she provided this for them. Reaction of the parents to their daughter's and son's disclosures was one of anger toward their eldest son, who they believed had taken advantage of his younger siblings. The father in the D family felt that his eldest son had betrayed his trust. He became emotionally distant from the boy, withdrawing affection and privileges that Brian had gained being the eldest child in the family. The mother, also angry at Brian, supported her husband in removing his privileges and in restructuring the parental roles in the family. She was able to share her anger about his behaviour clearly, but at the same time she was also able to show him that he had not lost her love and affection.

The boy appreciated his mother's support and was devastated by his father's reaction. He was worried that he would never regain his father's love and respect nor be able to resume his special status as the eldest child in the family. It was difficult for the father to believe that Lisa had, in any way, initiated sex play in the first stages of this sexual interaction with her brother. Although the mother accepted the view that her daughter had a part in the initiation of the sexualized play, she did not expect her young daughter to be held in any way accountable. This was one of the most difficult issues for the young offender to deal with. He seemed to be confused by the conflicting messages he was receiving from his mother. That is, she seemed to agree that his sister had some initial responsibility, but at the same time her statements indicated that she believed he was to be blamed entirely for the situation.

It was the case manager's opinion that the young offender in this family had had a great deal of responsibility thrust upon him early in his life. His parents, especially his father, had high expectations of him, both in school and in sports. He appeared to be 'over-responsible' for his age. On the other hand, the eldest girl in the family, although four years older than the twins, seemed developmentally about the same emotional age as her youngest siblings. The parents appeared to treat her like an infant. They did not seem to expect her to be as responsible for her behaviour as her older brother, nor did they show as high expectations of her. Of all the children, the mother believed Lisa to be the most sensitive, the most in need of reassurance.

The case manager, at the outset of referral, made a decision to deal with all aspects of the case herself. The family was grateful to learn that only one therapist would be working with them and that counselling would begin immediately. After determining all the instances of inappropriate sexual activity within the family, the case manager clarified for all the family members, and repeatedly for the children, the steps the counselling would involve and the specific agendas that would be set for treatment. At this time, the family was told that the case manager would want to begin by talking with the whole family together, then individually with the victims, the offender, and the parents. Treatment would end with a number of sessions with the whole family together again.

The initial clinical hypothesis about the D family was that Brian's sexual activities with his younger sister and brother were 'affection based.' The therapist felt that Brian, by offending against his sister and younger brother, was expressing a need for more emotional involvement with his parents, while simultaneously disqualifying himself as a mature, responsible, 'elder' child. In essence, he had been given 'power' within the family inappropriate to his developmental age. Brian's behaviour, coupled with his sister's disclosure, initiated changes within the D family that signalled their need for help. It gave the parents an opportunity to reconsider their belief that Brian was a mature and responsible adult. Lisa's disclosure allowed her to be viewed as someone to be taken seriously. Finally, it highlighted the need for the father to be reunited with his family and discontinue his peripheral involvement.

The case manager set out to help the family develop new relationship patterns and restructure itself in the following ways:

1. A number of whole family sessions were held to enable the parents re-establish parental control and begin restructuring personal boundaries within the family. The couple were able to talk about and change certain specific family patterns and rituals. For example, rituals at bedtime (or on other occasions where dressing, undressing, or bathing happened) were reviewed and considered. Clear personal-privacy rules were set that directed the children to close the doors to the bathrooms and bedrooms while they were engaged in these kind of activities. The parents were firm with their eldest son in discussing the inappropriateness of his behaviour, and supported the two

victims when they disclosed about their brother. It was made known within the family that inappropriate sexual behaviours would not be tolerated, and that children should always tell their parents about such inappropriate touching.

2. Individual work with the victims validated their rights as separate persons. Therapy helped them learn and identify various emotions, show behaviour congruent with their feelings, and have trust in themselves.

3. Individual therapy with the perpetrator helped the boy identify his feelings of guilt and shame about behaving sexually with his sister and brother and being discovered. The therapist helped him to recognize and express his feelings of being hurt and angry at his parents, for the loss of respect and nurturing he experienced, and for the anger he felt towards his sister for betraying him. Time was spent helping him to separate issues of normal healthy sexuality from abusive sexuality, and further, to help him understand the impact he had on the people around him, especially the effects of the abuse on his sister and brother. The boy was helped to talk about the expectations placed on him by his parents. He was helped to begin dealing with his feeling that he was not receiving the positive emotional contact he wanted with his parents, especially his father.

4. Work with the parental subsystem indicated that patterns of spousal life were frequently organized around parent-child activities, usually as a family. This pattern not only interfered with the marital relationship, it blocked the possibility of the children forming individual autonomous relationships with the parent of each gender. The couple spent a great deal of time discussing issues of intimacy, spousal absenteeism, autonomy, and interdependence. Time was spent helping each parent talk about what their relationship to each child should be and how they planned to be together in a way that was different from the past.

Family therapy helped the family as a whole solidify boundary changes that were evolving as individual and subsystem therapy progressed. In addition, family members were able to express how they were beginning to see their family change as a new meaning of their life together emerged. The parents in the D family were very motivated to implement changes as a family, and quickly adopted an appropriate hierarchial stance with their children. This strengthened the boundaries between the two generations in the home and encouraged mutual responsibility and trust in the sibling subsystem. It also resulted in the father becoming more active and available emotionally to his wife and children. In general, a more balanced interdependence of the genders in the family resulted. When family therapy was terminated, the parents believed that all members of the family had grown stronger and become closer.

The fact that the D family was a 'voluntary family' that dealt openly with the sexual abuse and welcomed treatment made them unusual within the child sexual abuse project. Not only did the parents have little resistance to treatment services from the outset, they were able to implement changes in the structure of their family quickly, and to find new more positive ways to conduct their personal, family, and community interactions. The 'primary social service intervention' (Furniss 1983) was also not required as a concurrent service theme, because the safety and protection of the children in their natural home setting was confirmed early in the progress of this case. Therefore, coordination of services was focused entirely on the sequence of appropriate therapeutic interventions. In the service response to child sexual abuse, it is a luxury to have treatment as the sole and central service activity. The challenge of providing coordinated services is greatly magnified by the need to arrange interagency deliberation and come to an agreement on a comprehensive service plan – one that must usually interweave family treatment, child protection, and judicial concerns.

PART TWO

Evaluation of Coordinated Child Sexual Abuse Services

6

The Manitoba Rural Child
Sexual Abuse Project

Participating Communities, Agencies, and Clients

Two geographic areas were selected to be included in the Manitoba Rural Child Sexual Abuse Project: South-Central Manitoba as the intervention or 'test' community, and South-Eastern Manitoba as the 'comparison' site. The coordinated treatment model was implemented in the test community while regular interagency services, as they were usually delivered, were monitored in the comparison community. The boundaries for the test and comparison communities were consistent with those of the two child protection agencies serving the geographic locales included in the project.

This chapter describes the two communities, giving the characteristics of the population of each. The two child welfare agencies that participated are described and compared, and a brief description of other human service agencies participating in the test community is provided. Finally, we offer a comparison of the clients and circumstances in the alleged sexual abuse cases that occurred in the two project communities over the one-year assessment period.

The Project Communities

The test area, or that geographic locale served by the south team of Child and Family Services of Central Manitoba, covers a large segment of the south-central region of Manitoba. The total population of the area, as indicated in the 1986 census, is 52,249. Approximately one half of the population is Anglo-Saxon. There is a large Mennonite population and large clusters of francophone residents. The economy of the region is agriculturally based and generally affluent. However, there are many examples of the two extremes: very affluent and very poor. The area has a strong religious flavour; the two principal religions are Mennonite and Catholic. The area is mainly rural, and contains a few larger towns including Winkler, Morden, Carman, Morris, and Altona.

The Latin-American Mennonite population merits special attention. It is composed of second and third generation families whose parents and grandparents left Canada in the 1930s to avoid the constraints imposed on them by the larger society at that time (e.g., compulsory education for their children and conscription). Today they are returning to Canada because Mexico has eliminated dual citizenship and introduced conscription. However, they continue to travel frequently between Mexico and Canada. They speak Low German and Spanish. In addition to the group from Mexico, other Mennonites are immigrating to the area from Paraguay and Bolivia. The Latin-American Mennonite population is quite insular and not well integrated into the wider Mennonite community.

The comparison area, or that served by the south team of Child and Family Services of Eastern Manitoba, extends across the bulk of south-eastern Manitoba. The population of the area, as indicated in the 1986 census is 36,120. The area is similar to south-central Manitoba in terms of ethnic groupings, and there is also a large number of Latin-American Mennonites, though there is a larger population of Paraguayan Mennonites in the comparison area. This group travels back and forth between Paraguay and Canada. The economy is also largely agriculturally based and fairly affluent, especially around larger towns such as Steinbach. The area includes a number of small towns, such as St. Adolphe and Ile Des Chênes, which are primarily commuting communities (i.e., the people live in the area but travel regularly to the large urban centre of Winnipeg for employment, shopping, and social activities).

Comparison of Communities

The characteristics of the population in the comparative study sites are highly similar. Table 6.1 presents a comparison of the two areas with regard to a number of social demographic variables. The test area does have a larger population and covers a wider area, but proportions of key social demographic variables are closely similar

Table 6.1   Population characteristics in comparative research sites

	Central		Eastern	
Total population (1986)	52,249		36,120	
Land area (km^2)	10,074		6,248	
Married/separated households	25,885		17,705	
Total number of families	13,140		9,090	
Number single-parent families	465		570	
Children by age:				
Under 6	5,195	(28%)	3,805	(28%)
6–14	7,705	(42%)	5,950	(42%)
15–17	2,555	(14%)	1,930	(14%)
18–24	2,960	(16%)	2,165	(16%)
Family incomes:				
0–9,999	975	(8%)	650	(7%)
10,000–19,999	3,585	(29%)	2,065	(23%)
20,000–29,999	3,190	(26%)	2,120	(23%)
30,000–39,999	2,060	(17%)	1,840	(20%)
40,000–49,999	1,250	(10%)	1,080	(12%)
50,000+	1,350	(11%)	1,360	(15%)
Average number of persons per household	2.97		3.19	
Average number of children per family	1.47		1.59	
Average number of persons per family	3.78		3.86	
Proportion of single-parent families	0.06		0.06	
Proportion born in Manitoba	0.80		0.81	
Proportion of adult males unemployed to employed	0.03		0.04	
Proportion of adult females unemployed to employed	0.07		0.08	
Proportion of low-income families	0.15		0.13	
Proportion of elderly (65 years +)	0.14		0.11	

in each geographic locale. Thus, as indicated in Table 6.1, the proportions of children by age grouping and the proportions of families across income categories are consistent in the two areas. Proportions with regard to the number of children per family, single parent families, low income families, and unemployed adults are almost identical in both areas. In view of these comparisons, one may conclude that the two sites were closely matched with regard to key population variables.

The areas were also well matched in terms of human service resources. Each area was served by a separate child and family service agency with equivalent resources, a community mental health team, a family violence shelter, mental retardation services, a probation office, and police detachments. One difference between the areas was the availability of the staff of the Eden Mental Health Centre. The centre specializes in the treatment of members of the Mennonite communities in southern Manitoba. Although it was more available to those living nearby in the test area, it did provide some services to those living in communities in the comparison area. Its main catchment area is the Winkler-Morden section of south-central Manitoba.

We will now examine the two CFS agencies that were the central participants in this project, describing each and highlighting their similarities and differences.

The Child and Family Service (CFS) Agencies

Child and Family Services of Central Manitoba: The South Team

Child and Family Services of Central Manitoba was the sponsoring agency for the project. In existence since 1934, it is one of the more senior child welfare agencies in the province. It is a private, non-profit organization that gets 98 per cent of its funding from the government and 2 per cent from private sources such as the United Way and door-to-door campaigns. The 2 per cent funding generated privately is designated for the development of special programs for children living in the local area (i.e., the summer camp program) and is not used for normal provision of the statutory services funded by government. The agency is governed by a board of directors consisting of fifteen people elected from its general membership. Any adult resident of the area may become a member by paying one dollar. Currently there are 180 members. The board has two functions: to set policy, and to hire the executive director, who ensures that service delivery is efficient and responsible to the residents of the region.

Although the administrative structure of the agency is centralized, the provision of services is decentralized and divided among three service teams: the permanency planning team, a specialized group dealing with adoption and post-legal registration; the north team; and the south team. The north team services the City of Portage la Prairie and surrounding areas, providing protection and family support services. The south team, which housed the project, serves the southern part of the catchment area. This geographic region also encompasses four Indian reserves. In 1985 the provision of child welfare services to Native persons living on the reserves became the responsibility of independent Native child welfare agencies.

When the project was initiated, the south team of CFS Central Manitoba consisted of nine staff: one supervisor, five treatment workers, two protection workers and one foster-home worker. Soon after the project began, one of the treatment workers was shifted to a protection position because of an increased number of abuse allegations and higher demands on the abuse workers. The south team operates out of a 'specialist model' of child welfare rather than a 'generalist model;' that is, there are specific workers with investigative and child protection duties and others for services such as family support or foster care. They had moved to this division of duties partly out of the belief that the investigative and treatment roles were complex and that each demanded specialized training and expertise. (The advantages of such specialization are elaborated upon in Chapter 3.) Child welfare workers are required to live within the catchment area of the agency, although there are occasional exceptions to this rule. The main administrative centre for the south team, including files and clerical support, is located in Portage la Prairie. There are two satellite offices in the south-central region, one in Carman and one in Winkler. The work base of about half the workers is located in Carman; the other half in Winkler. Two of the workers live in Portage la Prairie; one lives in Winnipeg and commutes to the south-central community offices.

The team has been working together for a number of years to develop a shared philosophy to guide service delivery. They are all trained in family-systems theory and all attempt to practise with a systemic orientation to intervention. While protection and treatment roles are separated, the intervention philosophies held by each group of workers are similar. This enhances their ability to work well together to coordinate investigation and treatment services. Peer supervision, consultation opportunities, and professional development are encouraged and expected. The south team within Child and Family Services of Central Manitoba has a strong belief that providing treatment services is an important component of work in a child welfare setting. For purposes of our study, while some attention was paid to community development activities, especially in terms of connections with the Mennonite community, the major focus was on treatment rather than on community development.

Child and Family Services of Eastern Manitoba: The South Team

Child and Family Services of Eastern Manitoba is a private, non-profit agency with a similar mandate and funding base as CFS Central. It is also governed by a board of directors composed of people from the local community. The south unit of CFS of Eastern Manitoba serves a rural catchment area and consists of 7.25 workers: 1 supervisor, 3 statutory workers, 2.5 resource workers, and .75 outreach workers. The statutory workers function primarily in a child protection role and are responsible for administering the legal mandate that governs the agency. The resource workers provide family support services, programs deemed appropriate to local communities such as family education and resources. In addition, they handle intake services for children and families requiring mandated services, and they provide short-term counselling. In many ways their role is similar to that of family service workers in the test area. The south team of Child and Family Services of Eastern Manitoba provides services through three community resource centres that operate several days a week to decentralize service delivery and provide a base for community development activities. The south team also utilizes a foster home coordinator and has an adolescent resource program operating out of the main agency offices.

Comparison of the Two Teams

From the descriptions it can be seen that the two teams are proportionally similar in terms of staff resources. The central–south team is somewhat larger, which is to be expected in view of the larger population it serves. Both teams relate administratively to a main central office, but utilize community offices for service provision. Both teams follow a specialist model with a clear separation between protection work and family support work. The major difference between them is one of emphasis with regard to treatment services. At CFS of Central Manitoba a stronger emphasis is placed on direct treatment through the provision of counselling for individuals, couples, and families. CFS of Eastern Manitoba focuses more on community-development activities and prevention strategies. However, family support workers in both areas do provide services that span both direct treatment and community development.

Provincial Child Abuse Committees

Each CFS agency in the Province of Manitoba is required by leg-islation to maintain a child abuse committee that will review al-legations and monitor investigative activities on cases where an al-legation of child abuse has been made. A major role of the committee is to form an opinion about whether abuse has occurred. While a thorough discussion of the child abuse committee's role is beyond the scope of this chapter, it is important to note that each agency participating in the project had a responsibility to maintain a link with its local child abuse committee.

In the region served by CFS of Central Manitoba, the child abuse committee meets twice a month to review cases. The committee is chaired by the supervisor of CFS of Central Manitoba's south team and consists of representatives from the medical profession, the RCMP, the CFS board of directors, the school system, and other community service providers. The committee is active and often assumes a protective stance in its review of cases. For example, if the committee has questions regarding the steps followed by CFS in an investigation, they may request detailed information and have formal reviews completed on a case-by-case basis. In the area served by CFS of Eastern Manitoba, the child abuse committee was not yet well established when the study was initiated. Cases were pre-sented to a child abuse committee that monitors all areas served by CFS Eastern, including both rural locales and a segment of the City of Winnipeg. This committee operates out of the urban centre of Winnipeg and although their scope is wider in terms of the geo-graphic area covered, the committee's membership has a similar com-position to that in the test area.

Other Agencies Participating in the Test Area of the Project

Community Mental Health (CMH)

The CMH program was developed in 1975 through the provincial government's Department of Health. Its main function is to provide emergency assistance and support to people in the community who have psychiatric problems. The program has no mandate to provide crisis intervention in child sexual abuse cases, despite the high prev-alence of abuse survivors in the cases now seen by the mental health team. In the test area the CMH team consists of three adult mental health workers and one children's worker. The team uses a variety of treatment modalities, including behaviour modification, crisis intervention, and family therapy. Team members all have some training in family systems theory and all utilize peer supervision and consultation. The staff works out of four decentralized offices across the service catchment area.

Eden Mental Health Centre, which treats mainly adult clients, is a private facility funded jointly by the provincial government and the Mennonite church. There are 40 in-patient beds and approximately 2,000 outpatients receiving treatment at any one time. Staff includes nurses, psychologists, psychiatrists, social workers, and geriatric specialists. Individual, family, and group therapies are utilized. Eden has a strong commitment to spirituality, primarily in the Mennonite tradition. Eden's involvement in the project was made primarily through links with staff from the social work and psychology departments.

Community Corrections

Community corrections services consists of two community corrections officers located in the test area. Their mandate is to provide assessments, recommendations, and services for clients proceeding through the legal system. A major function is the preparation of preliminary disposition reports that provide the court with information and recommendations concerning offenders. The community corrections officers in the area were peripherally involved in the project. They irregularly attended treatment committee meetings, but did participate in case management meetings as necessary.

South Central Committee on Family Violence

This organization, started in 1984, has three purposes: (1) to promote a public awareness of the violence that occurs within families; (2) to provide information to caregivers and the community in general about helpful ways of dealing with victims and offenders, and to encourage collective community action to deal with family violence; and (3) to provide programs and services designed to meet directly the needs of victims of abuse. It operates a crisis shelter for battered women and their children and offers a number of nonresidential services (i.e., support groups, counselling, and a twenty-four-hour toll-free crisis line). The committee is staffed by nine workers, each of whom participated in the project to varying degrees.

Mental Retardation

This program consists of two major services, one directed towards adults and one towards children. The primary goal of the adult service is to habilitate and rehabilitate qualifying adults and provide them with necessary supports in what could be considered a 'least restrictive environment.' The children's service is responsible for the planning and development of innovative programming for disabled children. The primary intent of this service is to assist disabled children and members of their families to enhance positive, long-term home care. These services function under the aegis of the Manitoba Department of Family Services and are operated province-wide. Two workers from Mental Retardation Services were involved in the project.

Police

The test area included seven RCMP detachments and three town police constabularies. In total there are approximately eighty police officers serving in this geographic area.

Having offered background information that describes the close similarities in the two comparative communities and agencies involved in the project, we will now turn our attention to the clients participating in the study and to the circumstances of intrafamilial child sexual abuse that were seen over a one-year period of service monitoring.

Clientele Involved in the Project

Inclusion criteria for the project called for: (i) cases involving an alleged offender who is either a member of the victim's family or who has been acting in a position of trust in the role of parent or caregiver to the child (e.g., clergy, teacher); (2) victims aged no more than eighteen years, and (3) cases where the allegations (as judged by the child welfare protection worker) have been either 'determined' (i.e., defined as confirmed by a guilty plea by the perpetrator) or 'probable' (i.e., defined as substantiated by one or more indicative signs). Selection criteria excluded cases that were 'uncertain' (i.e., defined as unsubstantiated by available evidence but not disproved) and cases determined to be 'unfounded' (i.e., defined as showing no evidence of sexual abuse, including suspicious behaviour or physical findings explainable by other causes).

All children and their families who met these criteria and from whom written, informed consent was obtained were included in the service-delivery and data-collection phase of the project from 1 February, 1989 to 31 January, 1990. Families who did not consent to participate in the study received the regular, ongoing services provided by Child and Family Services to cases involving allegations of child sexual abuse. However, no service impact or outcome measures were collected from them.

Cases Served: Client and Situational Characteristics

Over a one-year period, forty-one disclosures of child sexual abuse were made in the test community and twenty-nine in the comparison area. Informed, written consents to participate in the research were secured from twenty-nine or 69 per cent of non-offending parents in the test locale and seventeen or 59 per cent in the comparison locale. When analysis was done of aggregated service information comparing the cohorts that consented to participate in the research with those that did not, few differences were found that might suggest bias in the study sample. There were no social demographic differences between those who participated and those that did not, with regard to size of family, employment status of household heads, proportions of families in which mothers were full-time homemakers, or ages of mothers. However, approximately 20 per cent of the disclosures came from households headed by single-parent mothers. It did appear that these mothers were likely to wish to participate (thirteen of a possible fourteen consented to be study subjects), as they seemed to welcome any additional resources they might secure in coping with their family situation.

There were no differences between those who consented and those who did not with regard to assaults by biological fathers, stepfathers, siblings, extended family members, or trusted third parties. There were no differences in the proportion of cases that involved intercourse, manual – genital stimulation, or fondling. Proportions of female victims and affiliation of victims with predominant local cultural groups (i.e., Caucasian, Latin-American Mennonite, Native) were no different in the two groups. Both consenting and non-consenting cases involved assaults that extended for an average period of ten to eleven months. A relationship was found between the age of onset of the abuse and whether or not a parent elected to participate in the project. That is, parents of children assaulted at a younger age tended to take part in the study more often, with less than 15 per cent of our overall sample involving children with onset of abuse in adolescence. Most families that had children that were first assaulted in their teenage years (seven of nine cases) did not consent to participate.

Comparing Clients in Test and Comparison Communities

Few differences were found in the social demographic characteristics of the clients served in the test area as compared to those in the comparison area. In terms of family circumstances, there were no statistically significant differences in the two comparative groups with regard to family size, proportions of single-parent households, proportions of mothers identified as full-time homemakers, proportions of mothers in full-time employment, proportions of fathers in full-time employment, or ages of fathers. Mothers in the comparison area were found to be significantly older than mothers in the test area. However, in substantive terms, both groups of mothers represented women in their thirties.

It was interesting to note that although there were no significant differences in the average number of children in families from these two comparative locales, it did appear that study families overall were large in size: an average of three children per family in the test area and four children per family in the comparison area. There were two predominant cultural groups equally dispersed in the test and comparison areas: Caucasian (approximately 60 per cent) and Latin-American Mennonite (approximately 25 per cent). Although the differences were not great enough to reach statistical significance, it did appear that the test area contained more economically disadvantaged people; there was both a greater proportion of single-parent households and two-parent families that had lower proportions of fathers in full-time employment. The families identified through disclosures of child sexual abuse in both geographic locales were represented by a large proportion (50 per cent) of traditional households containing mothers who worked as full-time homemakers.

The Children

Child behaviour profiles generated through parent reports on the Achenbach Child Behaviour Checklist (Achenbach & McConaughy 1987; Achenbach & Edelbrock, 1983) were compared for victims from the test and comparison locales. Twenty-eight victims were assessed including sixteen in the six-to-eleven age range and ten in the twelve-to-sixteen age range.[1] Different norms are available for these age groups, so they were analysed separately. A statistical comparison revealed that there were no significant differences on the Activities, Social, or School sub-scales of social competence for either age group when children from the comparison and test areas were compared. Further, none of the nine sub-scales of the Revised Child Behaviour Profile for children aged six to eleven were found to be significantly different in the comparative groups, nor were the eight sub-scales of the profile for children aged twelve to sixteen. Averaged scores for all children between the ages of six and eleven, included in this study, for which the Achenbach scale was completed, appeared to be within the normal range on all sub-scale scores. Although the children between the ages of twelve and sixteen appeared to be similarly within the normal range for social competence scores, average scores were in the abnormal range of psychological functioning for anxious obsessive behaviour, somatic complaints, depressed withdrawal, and cruel behaviours. That is, the older children tended to show more types and severity of psychological symptomatology than the younger ones at the time of disclosure of child sexual abuse.

---

[1] Two of the assessed victims were in the four-to-five age range. Because of the small size of this sub-sample, no comparative analyses were attempted between the test and comparison areas for these young children.

Characteristics of the Abuse Situation

No statistically significant differences were found when character-istics of the abuse situation were compared in the two geographic locales. Therefore, prevalence rates during the one-year study period are reported here as averages across both participating communities. These averaged rates are likely the most accurate given the small numbers of subjects involved over the limited study time period.

Since most cases reported here were in the early phases of in-vestigation and treatment, few had completed court proceedings. Therefore, the descriptions of perpetrators and their actions that follow is largely based on those cases in which the abuse is alleged but not confirmed. The most prevalent perpetrator was the bio-logical father involving approximately one-third of all cases. Sibling incest accounted for 23 per cent of the disclosed sexual assaults. Extended family assaults (including members with step-family sta-tus) represented one-quarter of the identified cases. Assaults that involved trusted-third-party situations (i.e., babysitters, clergy, or teachers) were found about 20 per cent of the time. Age of per-petrators averaged thirty-three years with a range of twelve to seventy-three years. A large proportion of the alleged perpetrators (73 per cent) flatly denied that the sexual abuse had occurred at the time of the disclosure.

Less than half of the victims (41 per cent) expressed confidence in the ability of the non-offending parent(s) to protect them from further sexual abuse. Approximately 10 per cent of victims were fearful at the time of disclosure and did not feel safe or protected in the home. One-third of the non-offending parents denied that the sexual abuse had occurred when the disclosure was first made. Investigative child welfare workers believed that about half (56 per cent) of the non-offending parents did not know that the sexual abuse had occurred at the time of the disclosure.

The average age of the child victim at the onset of sexual abuse was eight years. Two-thirds of the cases were between the ages of four and twelve. Twenty-five per cent of the cases were five years old or younger, and 10 per cent were teenagers at the onset of the abuse. The average duration of the abuse prior to disclosure was ten to eleven months, with approximately half of the cases in-volving abuse that was more than one year in duration. Seventeen per cent were single-episode assaults on a child. Victims were pre-dominantly female (90 per cent).

Fondling of body areas that were not genital in location was involved in approximately 20 per cent of the cases, manual stimulation of the genitals in 44 per cent of the cases, and vaginal or anal intercourse accounted for 38 per cent of the sexual assaults.

No overt coercion was found in approximately one case in five at the time of the sexual assault. When coercion was used, the most common methods were the exercise of a position of authority (46 per cent), the threat of loss of affection (36 per cent) and the use of physical force (24 per cent). No overt coercion was found to be used to maintain secrecy about the sexual abuse in 24 per cent of the cases. In instances in which coercion was used to maintain secrecy, a number of methods were reported. The most common involved an appeal to family loyalty (40 per cent) or the threat of family loss (10 per cent), the threat of physical force or violence (14 per cent), the abuse of a position of authority (25 per cent), and the threat of loss of affection (14 per cent).

Four situational factors appeared to be present in similar proportions with respect to child sexual abuse cases in both study locales: (1) the abuse occurred while a child victim was visiting the home of the perpetrator (i.e., in 30 per cent of those instances in which the perpetrator lived elsewhere), (2) physical abuse was concurrently present with the child sexual abuse (14 per cent), (3) alcohol abuse was identified as an element in the child sexual abuse (27 per cent), (4) conditions of poverty were seen as playing a central role in the child sexual abuse (10 per cent).

Social Network Attributes of Cases on the Two Study Sites

Detailed social network measures were completed at the initiation of service delivery for 33 or 72 per cent of the families who had given their informed consent as research participants. Non-offending mothers served as the source of information concerning family social resources. A systematic interview protocol was followed to secure measures of social network size and dimensionality. A wide range of social network information was collected. Parents identified family members and friends with whom they had regular contact and whom they felt they could turn to for various kinds of help. No ceiling on network size was imposed. Network dimensionality (i.e., the type of network support provided) was assessed for each person identified. The approach used was modeled after

Hirsch (1980), McCannell Saulnier (1984), and Oritt, Paul, and Behrman (1985).

Families in which a child was sexually abused were found to have small social networks. On average, mothers had contact with six family members (including nuclear and extended family networks). On average, mothers had contact with four friends and two human-service professionals at the time of the disclosure. The numbers of family members, friends, and professionals that provided support to the study families were closely consistent with the network membership sizes previously reported for families with a child at risk for out-of-home placement (McCannell Saulnier & Rowland 1985).

The different types of social support provided by the different people (including spouse) within the family network included helping with household tasks (3.5 persons), participation in social activities (4 persons), giving advice (3.5 persons), listening to worries (4 persons), offering emergency help (3.5 persons), acting as a trusted confidante (3 persons). These family networks were therefore generally found to be sparse sources of social support. The different types of social support provided by friends, included helping with household tasks (1.5 persons), showing social activities (2.5 persons), giving advice (2 persons), offering emergency help (1.5 persons), acting as personal confidante (1 person). Like the family network, the friendship network appeared to be a sparse source of social support.

The previous measures taken to provide actual social support were supplemented with a measure that would tap aspects of perceived social support: the Revised UCLA Loneliness Scale (Russell, Peplau, & Cutrona 1980). Parents from the comparison area were found to be no different in their level of perceived loneliness than parents in the test community. Further, these parent scores on the Loneliness Scale were found to be no different than the normative means of this scale, suggesting that they did not perceive themselves to be any more lonely than members of the normative group.

A Summary of Comparability of Cases in Test and Comparison Locales

A review was done of key client and social demographic characteristics in families that consented to complete treatment outcome measures and those that did not, but few differences were found.

Regarding most social demographic characteristics and key elements of the sexual abuse situation, it did appear that there was no respondant attribute that suggested sampling bias because of refusals to participate. However, it did seem that parents of children with disclosures of sexual abuse at younger ages (the pre-teen years) were more likely to agree to participate in the study. It seemed that children who were sexually assaulted during their teenage years were identified to the service system less frequently in both study communities than what one might expect. When they were involved with community agencies at the time the sexual abuse was disclosed, they and their family members seemed less accepting of professional involvement. Thus, identification, investigation, and treatment of teenage victims seems to be an aspect of child sexual abuse services that warrants special study.

Two features that were consistent across test and comparison areas in this project – features that might limit the range to which study findings might be generalized to apply to other families in which incest has occurred – involved the size and economic status of families. Overall, families participating in the research tended to be larger in size; on average, three children per family. As well, there seemed to be an over-representation of families in lower income groups. It is not clear whether these family attributes might in some way mediate the impact of a coordinated treatment approach, or whether they are inconsequential to the ongoing delivery of investigative and treatment services in situations of intrafamilial child sexual abuse.

Overall, remarkable similarities were found to exist in the two comparative research groups. On all key social demographic characteristics the two community groups seemed closely matched. Further, when situational circumstances, attributes of victims, and characteristics of perpetrators were assessed, the two comparative groups of cases appeared to be closely similar at the onset of the project. These findings, coupled with the information gathered on comparative community characteristics, provide strong argument that this study did involve two well matched comparison groups. That is, the study groups are closely matched with regard to (1) similarity of cases, including characteristics of victim, perpetrator, and non-offending parent; (2) the social demographic characteristics of family units entering the service system; and (3) the macro-environmental circumstances of each of the communities in which the study families reside.

Unusual Features of the Child Sexual Abuse Cases Reported across Both Rural Study Communities

Caution must be exercised when interpreting, over one year, the prevalence rates of a study variable that is reported in a community in only very limited numbers. For example, with incest, which is reported in only a small percentage of the population, one could have more confidence in prevalence rates that were collected continuously over a long time period or that were repeated in a large number of comparative communities. Unfortunately very little epidemiological information has been reported relating to the prevalence of incest specifically in rural communities. The statistical consistency in the numbers of both children and abuse characteristics in the two rural communities taking part in the project (each separately and independently reported) suggested that our prevalence rates could be trusted. However, when we compared some of the key incest circumstances with epidemiological findings reported earlier, there were several marked differences that warranted careful consideration.

Baseline epidemiological statistics were taken from Kroth (1979), whose collection of epidemiological information on child sexual abuse is to date the most extensive information based on monitoring of community services (although it is also based on a cross-section of rural and urban California locales). Our data collection forms were modelled on the system Kroth designed to evaluate the well recognized Child Sexual Abuse Treatment Program (CSATP) based on Giarreto's (1976) treatment model. Two findings in particular were unexpected: the predominance of younger child victims in the project caseloads and the high proportion of cases involving vaginal or anal penetration. In the CSATP approximately one-third of the cases involved teenagers, while this age group represented only 10 per cent of our study cohort of rural children. In the CSATP 13 per cent of reported cases involved vaginal or anal penetration, while 38 per cent of our cohort of rural children suffered this extent of physical invasion.

More recent service tracking (Levitt, Owen, and Truchsess 1991) has been done to evaluate child sexual abuse services from 1985 to 1986 in the upper midwest region of the State of Minnesota in the United States, (a neighbour of the Province of Manitoba). The cases reviewed included those from both urban and rural communities that were seen at the primary assessment unit serving the region at the Children's Hospital in Saint Paul, Minnesota. However, the Minnesota service review created a rare opportunity for us to compare our prevalence rates with more recent, systematically collected information on child sexual abuse victims. The Minnesota cohort was more consistent with our own, both in terms of the age of the children at the time of disclosure and the time the sexual abuse ended (only 18 per cent of these children were over the age of ten). In terms of extent of the violation, 22 per cent of the Minnesota children suffered anal or vaginal penetration. These findings are more in line with our own than those in Kroth's report involving the CSATP.

We interpret the differences in the ages and numbers of victims suffering anal or vaginal penetration to several overlapping circumstances. First, our project involved solely rural communities. As we have previously noted, there is a greater sense of protectiveness and secrecy in these communities because of the social closeness of the sparse networks of people in these locales. Further, our study communities were distinctive in their conservative political attitudes and fundamentalist religious beliefs. We believe these socio-cultural factors would tend to create a predisposition in community members to minimize or deny signals of potential sexual abuse.

Most professionals investigating child sexual abuse will admit there is often a fine line between fondling and affectionate caressing, which creates difficulties in determining whether an allegation of abuse can be substantiated. In our study communities, where the identification of abuse has such powerful social, economic, and legal repercussions, it seems likely that these cases that are clearly serious in terms of their physical intrusion on a child are more likely to be formally recognized. We believe that is a major reason why a large proportion of the disclosures involved aggressive and extensive assaults on children. As well, it is important to acknowledge that Kroth's statistics concerning prevalence of sexual abuse were collected some sixteen years ago, and that much has changed since then, particularly in terms of preventative programs in the elementary school systems. Manitoba and Minnesota are two geographic locales in which there has been a serious commitment to preventative programs in elementary school systems. We believe that the increase in proportions of younger children with disclosures of sexual abuse is tied to earlier and more sensitive recognition in the schools, churches, and health care facilities.

The low numbers of teenagers being reached by services in our rural study communities is, however, a troubling situation. Rural child welfare investigators are cognisant of this issue and are perplexed by the frequency with which teenage victims will recant when formal disclosures are made. It seems that teenagers, living in families in which they are incest victims, are becoming more aware of the high social and family costs involved in pursuing this issue through the child welfare system and the courts. It seems that they are also becoming increasingly aware that, after all the disruption and pain both to themselves and their family members, disclosures often do not result in adequate resolution of their family's distress and their own sexual victimization. In our study communities, churches were one sector of the rural community that seemed to be growing more aware of these troubling circumstances. In our study sites there were a number of disclosures to church staff by teenaged victims (e.g., to pastors or to Bible Camp counsellors) that were subsequently denied by the teenage victims when child welfare investigators or police were contacted. It does seem that the rural churches are growing in their realization that they might be the only ones entrusted with a victim's disclosure, and that they need to learn to help victims reach further for help from others (i.e., from mandated authorities such as the police and child welfare agencies).

Much work remains to be done to introduce prevention programs in schools, churches, and other important community settings to help children and youth protect themselves from sexual exploitation. Secondary prevention programs should be mobilized to help already victimized children gain access to the services they need. These programs should be especially focused for sexually abused children who believe it is best to avoid detection, or who feel pressured, after disclosure, to recant and escape investigation.

7

Coordinated Community Services

Staff Resources and Their Deployment

The coordinated community service approach requires a high level of commitment from professionals providing direct services to clients. The people-power or hours-of-service effort required to maintain such coordinated systems are not trivial and cannot be met through simple juggling of existing staff in the participating agencies.

To track service activities in a coordinated service system responding to child sexual abuse in a rural setting, careful monitoring of service delivery patterns was maintained over the one-year, service delivery phase of our project.

Patterns of Service Delivery

During the one-year period from 1 February 1989 to 31 January 1990 all service contacts relating to child sexual abuse were monitored in the test and comparison locales. Members of the child and family service teams, all serving in the two catchment areas included in the project, completed a service record whenever they had contact with a client or with a collateral professional on behalf of a client (e.g., police, a physician). Members of the treatment committee in the test area completed these forms to track all treatment services. This included all local agencies serving as treatment providers (e.g., child and family, mental health, and family violence services). All face-to-face episodes of service and telephone service contacts were recorded.

Figure 7.1
Total contacts by all CFS workers:
Comparing test and comparison areas

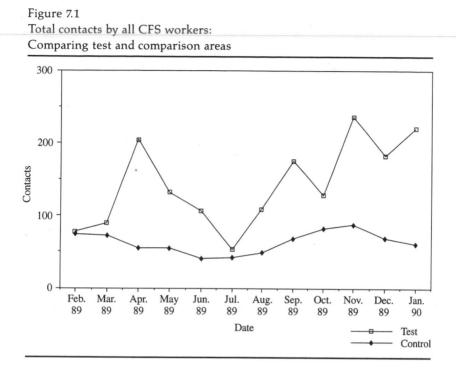

An Overview of Service Contacts by Child and Family Service Workers in the Two Comparative Communities

The total number of service contacts relating to intrafamilial child sexual abuse delivered by members of the two comparative CFS teams are presented above, in Figure 7.1.

The team within the comparison community showed a pattern of service delivery (monthly contacts) that remained at approximately the same level of monthly contacts through the one-year period of service monitoring, although there were seasonal variations (a service slow-down during the summer months). The test community, in which the coordinated service model was implemented, showed a steadily increasing number of service contacts. This increase in the test area reached statistical significance (meaning that the size of the increase in service for child sexual abuse could not have happened by chance).

Figure 7.2
Client contacts by all CFS workers:
Comparing test and comparison areas

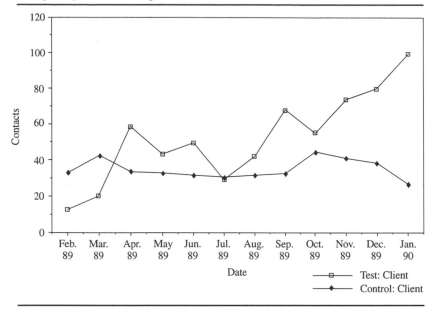

There was a dramatic rise in the number of contacts in the test area during the month of April and a marked decrease during the month of July. The April surge in services was found to be tied to the disclosure of child sexual abuse in three families that required unusually high levels of involvement by professional caregivers. Families such as these will emerge on a case-by-case basis at different times during the year. However, it was extraordinary to have three of these 'heavy service users' identified in the same month. The drop in service contacts during the summer months was likely directly related to summer vacations taken by child welfare personnel, and by the collateral professionals with whom they worked.

The overall service patterns by child welfare personnel were considered separately, because they related to 'direct contacts' with clients and to 'indirect contacts' with collateral human service professionals. The direct client contacts are presented in Figure 7.2 and indirect collateral contacts in Figure 7.3.

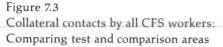

Figure 7.3
Collateral contacts by all CFS workers:
Comparing test and comparison areas

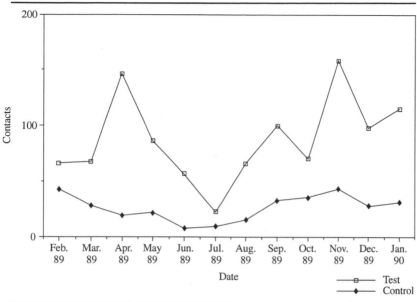

One would anticipate that there would be greater numbers of client contacts in the test area because its population was larger. During the first two months of the project, the number of clients in the test area increased to a range that would be expected considering the population served, relative to the population served in the comparison area. The test area had fewer disclosures, and open cases prior to the initiation of the research project.[1] However, there was a steady rise in the number of cases opened in the test area throughout the course of the project. The differences found in the level of service contacts with clients, across the one year service-tracing period, were significantly higher in the test area than in the comparison area. The increase in the number of contacts

---

[1] This was confirmed by a retrospective file audit which revealed that for the two years preceding the initiation of the project, fewer intrafamilial child sexual abuse cases were reported in the test area.

with collateral professionals (or other professionals involved in services to the client) did not increase as dramatically for the entire
CFS team as did direct client contacts (see Table 7.3, p. 147).

It was interesting to note that the shape of the line graph for
collateral contacts was closely similar to that for the overall service
patterns. The high peak of service in the month of April and the
low level of contacts in July seemed to be more closely related to
the variations in the numbers of collateral contacts made by the
CFS staff. That is, client contacts tended to remain more consistent
on a month-to-month basis, while the collateral contacts seemed
to have more seasonal variations.

Service Contacts by Child and Family Service Workers Investigating Allegations of Child Sexual Abuse in the Two Comparison Communities

The decision to focus the study of client contact intensively on a
one-year period led us to monitor services that largely related to
the investigations of disclosures of child sexual abuse. Only the
early phases of the treatment process could be initiated in most cases
seen during this period of service tracking.

Since there was an emphasis on service delivery that was initiated
close to the time of the disclosures of child sexual abuse, and on
the subsequent investigative process that ensued, it was important
to track closely the activities of the CFS investigative workers on
each of the teams included in the project. Each of the teams had
three workers who primarily held staff positions as abuse investigators. The proportion of child sexual abuse cases carried by each
of the three investigative workers in both comparative sites were
balanced. These workers shared investigative duties for all abuse
and neglect disclosures in their geographic areas. It did appear that
similar caseloads of child sexual abuse cases occurred in both teams.

Although staff resources in the two teams were equivalent, the
population base served was greater in the test area, in which the
coordinated community model was implemented. Over the one-year
period, it did appear that the cases served in the two sites were
what one would expect relative to the size of their respective populations. Over the one-year review period, the test team averaged
13.3 cases per month and the comparison team 10.8 cases. The ratio
of the *population size* in the two catchment areas was 1: 1.40 (com-

parison to test) and the ratio of the *numbers of cases investigated* was 1: 1.41 (comparison to test). However, the ratio of service contacts by investigative workers in the two sites was 1: 1.88 (comparison to test). The test team averaged 114 service contacts related to child sexual abuse cases per month, while the comparison team averaged 61 per month. This difference was statistically significant.

In terms of direct service contacts made solely with clients, the test team averaged 38.8 client contacts per month and the comparison team 34.3 contacts. The difference in the average number of client contacts per month did not reach statistical significance.

It did appear that even with the more limited staff resources, the test team did maintain, over the one-year period, a higher level of service contacts per case when investigating disclosures of child sexual abuse. It also appeared that these higher levels were the result of the test team's more active work with collateral professionals – that is, the work it did on behalf of, rather than directly with, its clients. This pattern was to be expected. In the locale with a coordinated treatment approach, one would anticipate that collateral contacts would rise dramatically while client contacts would remain relatively stable, particularly during the investigative and early-treatment phases of service delivery.

Three aspects of service delivery by investigative workers will be more closely reviewed: service contacts with clients (Figure 7.4), service contacts with other child welfare personnel (Figure 7.5), and service contacts with professionals from other community agencies (Figure 7.6).

In a visual comparison of service contacts with clients, per investigative worker, in each of the two study communities, one can see a more prominent rise in the numbers of contacts in the test area during the first two months of the project (see Figure 7.4). After this, the levels of service delivery, as these relate to direct client contacts, continue a steady increase. When one considers the *rate* of increase of client contacts over the full one-year period, the test area shows an increase in client contacts that is significantly greater than in the comparison area.

During the term of this project, one of the evident differences between the two study sites was the number of contacts investigative workers made with other child welfare workers on their CFS team (see Figure 7.5). In the comparison area there was only infrequent consultation or information exchange about child sexual abuse cases.

Figure 7.4
Service contacts with clients by investigative workers:
Comparing test and comparison areas

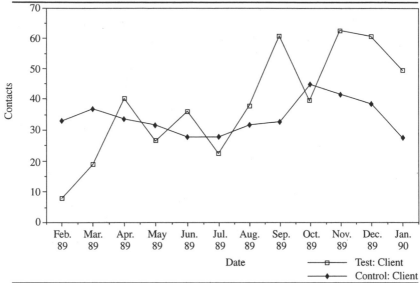

The investigative workers in the comparison community tended to work independently during the investigation of an allegation of sexual abuse, and treatment services were largely offered by professionals outside their child welfare agency. In contrast, in the test community there was heightened treatment involvement by child welfare personnel within the same agency as the investigative worker. As the project progressed, consultation between child welfare personnel increased in frequency as coordinated services included more consultation between those identified as 'protection' workers and those identified as 'treatment workers.' When one considers the *rate* of increase of collateral contacts within the child welfare agencies, the rate of increase was significantly higher in the test site. As well, the average number of internal agency collateral contacts made on a month-to-month basis over the one-year research period was significantly higher in the test area than in the comparison area.

Right from the start of the project, the investigative workers in the test area maintained a higher level of collateral contacts with

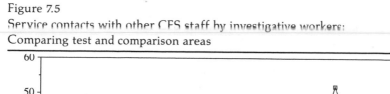

Figure 7.5
Service contacts with other CFS staff by investigative workers:
Comparing test and comparison areas

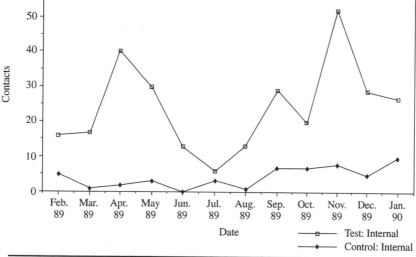

professionals from other human service agencies in their community. Although these contacts were reduced over the summer
months, they did remain at a higher level relative to that maintained
by the investigative workers in the comparison area. When compared
across sites, monthly contacts in both locales remained relatively
constant. When analysed on a month-by-month basis, study-area
team members maintained a significantly higher level of collateral
linkages, with an average of 51.1 external agency contacts, than
comparison team members who maintained an average of 22.3 such
contacts. Collateral service contacts with professionals from other
community agencies are shown in Figure 7.6.

Child Welfare Investigative Workers: Service Patterns in the Two Study Sites

Although there were approximately twice as many service contacts
in the test area than in the comparison area over the one-year service
tracking period, there were significant differences in the *proportions*

Figure 7.6
Service contacts with outside agency staff:
Investigative workers in test and comparison areas

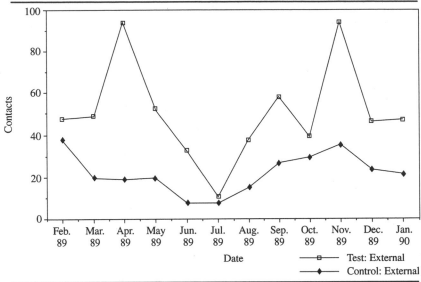

of service that involved contacts with clients, internal agency professionals, and external agency professionals (see Table 7.1). Direct client contacts represented 38 per cent of the investigative workers' service in the test area and 56 per cent in the comparison area. Collateral contacts with other agency social workers was found to be linked to 21 per cent of the service contacts in the test area and 7 per cent in the comparison area.

The greatest differences occurred in the proportions of service contacts that related to collateral linkages; that is, contacts with other professionals within the child and family service agency, and with professionals working in other community settings. This larger proportion of work, with collateral professionals within the same agency, appeared to be tied to development of treatment services. In the test community most treatment services were offered by staff within the CFS agency, while most treatment services in the comparison area were offered by community agencies external to CFS. The high level of internal CFS agency consultation in the test area is consistent with the development of internal agency

Table 7.1
Service contacts with clients and collaterals: A Comparison of investigative workers
in test and comparison areas

Count Row % Column %	Client	Internal collateral	External collateral
Test	466 34.0 53.1	292 21.3 84.9	614 44.8 69.7
Comparison	411 56.3 46.9	52 7.1 15.1	267 36.6 30.3

treatment services; that is, with a service structure that allowed family service workers to bridge with investigative workers as the cases progressed through the investigative phase. The higher levels of professional contact with personnel from agencies external to CFS were also consistent with the development in the test area of coordinated, interdisciplinary treatment services.

It should be noted that while collateral professional contacts were significantly higher in the test area, the numbers of client contacts were also maintained at a slightly higher level than those of the comparison team.

When the proportions of service provided by different professional groups in the community were considered, it was found that both test and comparison team members allocated the same proportions of time to each different discipline. The major professional groups with ongoing contact with investigative workers were the police and 'other' community professionals such as clergy, shelter staff, and teachers (see Table 7.2).

With regard to location of contacts, the investigative workers in the test area completed 56 per cent of their contacts with outside agency professionals in community settings (other than their offices) compared to 28 per cent by comparison team members. This difference was statistically significant. Further, 41 per cent of contacts with outside community professionals occurred on a direct, 'face-to-face' basis compared to 29 per cent in the comparison team. This difference was also statistically significant. When proportion of time allocated to contacts with professionals outside of the CFS

Table 7.2

Contacts with professionals from external human service agencies by investigative workers in test and comparison areas

Count Column %	Test	Comparison
Police	215 36.7	79 30.7
Physician	38 6.5	17 6.6
Mental Health	36 6.1	23 8.9
Legal	41 7.0	21 8.2
Social Services	37 6.3	14 5.4
Other	219 37.4	103 40.1

agency was reviewed, it was found that both teams spent equivalent amounts of time when they made collateral service contacts. However, there did appear to be a higher proportion of longer contacts (lasting one hour or more) by the comparison team members (see Table 7.3). This may have been related to their need to secure on-going treatment services that could only be obtained outside their agency setting.

In terms of service contacts made directly with clients, it was found that team members in the test area made 43 per cent of these contacts in community settings (other than their offices) compared to 30 per cent by members of the team from the comparison area. This difference was statistically significant. Although team members in the test area made slightly more face-to-face contacts as compared to telephone contacts (52 per cent) than comparison team members (50 per cent), these differences were not great enough to reach statistical significance.

When proportions of time spent in direct contacts with clients were considered in each of the two study sites, it was found that investigative workers in the test area tended to spend proportion-

Table 7.3
Time involved in service contacts with professionals from outside of agency:
Comparisons of CFS protection workers in test and comparison communities

Count Row %	10 minutes or less	11–29 minutes	30–59 minutes	One hour or more
Test	242 39.7	268 44.0	67 11.0	32 5.3
Comparison	103 39.0	108 40.9	26 9.8	27 10.2

ately more time in brief contacts and less in lengthy (over one hour) sessions with clients. Given the high level of collateral activity engaged in by these workers, it was not surprising that they were limited in the time they could allocate to client interviews. One could surmise that because investigative workers in the test site had easier access to treatment services in their local community, they could focus more time with clients on investigative matters. The comparison area investigative workers were pulled into more treatment-related issues, and that may account for the longer time spent with clients. As one investigative worker in the comparison area said, 'It's hard for me to know where treatment begins and investigations end.' Proportions of time spent with clients by investigative workers from the two study sites is shown in Table 7.4.

Considering the overall division of labour by investigative workers, significant differences were found in the teams of investigative workers from the test and comparison areas. Service delivery was considered according to five major types of sessions: emergency, investigative, treatment, information, and integrated investigative/treatment. The two sites differed significantly in the proportions of contacts allocated to these different service divisions, as presented in Table 7.5. The key areas of difference appeared to be in the proportions of service delivery allocated to investigation and treatment. A clear distinction was made that investigative workers in the test area were largely to do investigations, and that other designated treatment personnel would deliver services from their own agency or from outside community agencies. A greater proportion of their time could be thus designated primarily to meet investigative duties.

Table 7.4
Proportions of time spent in direct contacts with clients by investigative workers in test and comparison areas

Count Row %	10 minutes or less	11–29 minutes	30–59 minutes	60–119 minutes	Two hours or more
Test	116 16.9	307 44.6	162 23.5	79 11.5	24 3.5
Comparison	22 7.1	68 21.8	77 24.7	118 37.8	27 8.7

In the comparison locale, treatment resources were more difficult to access by investigative workers, and it did appear that there was a stronger pull for them to provide treatment service themselves (see Table 7.5).

Treatment Services in the Experimental Community Setting

Although the review of investigations – those tied to the disclosure of intrafamilial and trusted-third-party child sexual abuse – was initiated at the onset of the research project in February 1989, the newly identified cases did not begin to receive coordinated treatment services until two months later, in April. We thus had a ten-month 'window' through which to track the delivery of coordinated treatment resources in the test community. Over this ten-month period, twenty-two cases received treatment. Because this was early in the treatment process for the bulk of the cases identified within the term of the project, most of these cases had received only preliminary clinical intervention by the end of the service monitoring period.

Most service contacts involving clinical treatment, and which were delivered during the ten-month analysis period, were provided by social workers from Child and Family Services (69 per cent). Many professionals became involved as members of the community treatment team (described in Chapter 3), including seven child welfare workers, five community mental health staff, and three workers from other community service settings. However, during the first ten months of service delivery, six professionals provided 77 per cent of the treatment services to clients. Two of these limited their

Table 7.5
Service focus of contacts with clients and collaterals: CFS protection workers in test and comparison areas

Count Row %	Emergency	Investigate	Treatment	Information	Invest. & treatment
	16	476	515	488	32
Test	1.4	40.9	13.0	42.0	2.8
	9	178	178	276	28
Comparison	1.3	26.6	26.6	41.3	4.2

work to individual counselling, two worked with individuals and family subsystems, and two largely offered group therapy.

Analysis of Direct, Face-to-Face Contacts with Clients

Approximately one fifth (22 per cent) of all treatment services delivered went to victims, one quarter (26 per cent) to perpetrators, one-quarter (29 per cent) to non-offending parents, and one-fifth (21 per cent) to other family members or family subsystems. The treatment received by these different client target groups may be described as approximately one-half individual counselling (52 per cent), one-third group therapy (33 per cent), and 15 per cent conjoint dyadic or family system counselling. Perpetrators largely received individual counselling, victims individual counselling and group therapy in equal proportions, and non-offending parents almost twice as many group session contacts as individual therapy sessions.

Thirteen family units received individual counselling delivered largely (65 per cent) by four clinicians. Nine family units were involved in group therapy delivered by three workers. Eight family units received some conjoint therapy involving family sub-systems, delivered largely (64 per cent) by two therapists. Just under one treatment contact in ten (9 per cent) was delivered as a co-therapy session involving more than one therapist.

The modal time spent in individual counselling sessions was thirty to fifty-nine minutes (52 per cent), although over one-third of the sessions (37 per cent) lasted more than one hour. The bulk of the group therapy sessions (72 per cent) were one to two hours long.

About half (51 per cent) of the direct therapeutic contacts with clients took place in the office of the therapist, one-third (30 per cent) in offices of other human service agencies, just over one in ten (14 per cent) occurred in the home of the client, and one in twenty (5 per cent) was arranged in other community settings such as a church or coffee shop.

On average, each client contact usually required one collateral service contact with another human service professional. One-third (37 per cent) of all collateral professional contacts were made in order to coordinate treatment, almost half (43 per cent) were to transmit information relevant to the treatment process, and about one in five (16 per cent) were for clinical consultation. Most collateral contacts were conducted over the telephone. For every face-to-face meeting with a professional colleague, four contacts were made by telephone.

Analysis of All Collateral Contacts Tied to Client Treatment

Fourteen of the twenty-two cases receiving treatment services (64 per cent) involved ongoing collateral consultation during the period of treatment monitoring. There were 1.21 client treatment contacts for each collateral contact. One collateral contact in five (19 per cent) involved case treatment consultation, almost half of the collateral contacts (42 per cent) were for treatment coordination and one-third (34 per cent) for the exchange of treatment-related information. Two-thirds of all collateral contacts (74 per cent) were made over the telephone. Three-quarters of all telephone contacts required less than ten minutes to complete, and one-fifth of the telephone contacts (22 per cent) lasted from eleven to twenty-nine minutes. One-quarter (25 per cent) of all face-to-face contacts with collaterals lasted more than one hour per session. Face-to-face contacts with collateral professionals usually involved treatment consultation (41 per cent) or case coordination (43 per cent). Telephone contacts with collateral professionals usually involved case coordination (41 per cent) or the exchange of case information (42 per cent).

Comparing Treatment Activities in the Two Study Sites

One year after formal service tracking had been discontinued (December 1990), we requested follow-up interviews with all families that had consented to be research participants in the two comparative study sites. Twenty-six of a possible forty-six families (57 per cent) were located and agreed to be interviewed over the telephone.

We completed statistical comparisons of the salient victim and perpetrator characteristics of cases that were included in the follow-up interviews and those that were not. There appeared to be no statistically significant differences between respondents and non-respondents – age of victims at the time of the assault, the period of time over which sexual abuse occurred, the nature of the assaults (fondling, genital manipulation, or intercourse), age of the perpetrator, or status of the perpetrator (father or sibling).

Because non-offending parents were the primary providers of family information on follow-up, analysis was done to see if the respondents and non-respondents differed in psychological or social well-being at the time of abuse disclosure and service initiation. In this regard, it was found that there were no differences in levels of depression, social isolation, overall perception of family adjustment, traumatic stress reaction, or social desirability in the non-offending parents who consented to follow-up interviews, as compared to those who could not be located or who refused to participate.

Therefore, it did not appear that there was an obvious systematic bias in the sample of respondents that might distort the findings of the follow-up survey.

Central to our research was the comparison between the levels of treatment services secured for child sexual abuse cases in each of the test and comparison communities. Two aspects of treatment were found to be significantly different in both. The first related to group therapy. In the test area, treatment groups had been initiated for child victims. The development of group service was enhanced by the creation of the coordinated treatment team, because the groups were co-led by staff from different agencies. No such resources were available in the comparison area, although one child victim had been accepted for treatment in a group located in a nearby city some distance from the family home. As well, it was found that individual counselling had been initiated with most perpetrators in the test community (eleven out of thirteen cases required treatment), while a smaller proportion (three out of seven) had obtained some individual counselling services in the comparison community.

The test community also developed locally maintained group treatment resources for juvenile perpetrators, and all four of the young perpetrators – members of research families in the test community – were treated in this group. Two of the four had received individual therapy as well as treatment in a group. There were two juvenile perpetrators in the sample of cases from the comparison area and, as of the follow-up date, neither had received either individual or group treatment.

Overall, we found that after one year most families in the test community (71 per cent) had received some type of treatment service relating to child sexual abuse, whereas only a small proportion of families in the comparison community (29 per cent) had received any type of treatment.

Implications for Staff Resources

It is clear that the coordinated service model will require additional staff and resources. In our project's coordination model a child welfare agency was the central hub of the service system, and it was most evident that special program resources would be needed to support the expanded child welfare role. Most human services are now facing times of fiscal restraint. However, there has been a hugely expanding demand for child sexual abuse services over the past several decades, a demand that has paralleled the heightened and widespread community awareness of this serious social problem. Priority must be given to the provision of adequate resources for these acutely needed investigative and treatment services. In our model, this calls for increased resources across a number of key service sectors, in particular an expanded participation by rural child welfare agencies.

Certainly the coordinated service approach will require special developmental funding, as there will be 'initial hump costs' during its early years of implementation. The initial costs will largely be tied to interagency planning and the consultation process that is needed in creating a service infrastructure. In rural areas this will mean additional resources for consultation, training, and travel. As well, two key positions will need to be funded: the service coordinator and parent support worker. Once the system is operational, ongoing service costs will be tied to the expense of maintaining regular meetings of key service providers in the coordinated system.

Further, as preventative community programs strengthen (e.g., in schools and churches) and investigative services increase in efficiency, there will be heightened demands for basic and multidimensional treatment services.

It has been our experience that Canadian rural communities do contain capable and appropriate treatment resources, but that these are already stretched to their limit and are often concentrated on crisis services. A coordinated child sexual abuse service system within a rural community cannot depend on the goodwill of local service providers alone, but must be supported by adequate funding across child welfare, mental health, health and criminal justice sectors.

The long-term effects of child sexual abuse are costly for victims, families, and communities. This is a human services issue that cannot be met with a minimum-treatment approach in an era of financial cutbacks (Land 1986). It is a complex human problem that requires a complex solution. Our findings indicate that coordinated rural services can be implemented by drawing on existing community resources, but that special infrastructure costs must be provided. These modest but essential costs should be shared by authorities in the government departments that are responsible for the investigation and treatment of child sexual abuse.

Morrill (1976) concluded, from the extensive research and experience of the Department of Health, Education, and Welfare in the United States, that, 'service integration seldom reduces costs in the short term' and that 'increased program effectiveness is likely to be seen much earlier than a decrease in service costs' (p. 54). The preliminary findings of this project, as outlined in the next chapter, offer some evidence that coordinated systems are more effective in the short term, and appear to show promise of being beneficial as well in the long term.

8

Indicators of the Impact of Coordinated Community Services

Because of the high level of stress in victims and their families, at the time of disclosure and at the onset of investigative services, care had to be exercised with regard to the choice of appropriate service outcome measures and the manner in which these were introduced to recipients. It was a challenge to secure pre-treatment measures, as these had to be collected close to the time of the disclosure of child sexual abuse, a time when most children and their parents were in situational crisis and emotional turmoil. Several principles were followed in this regard:

First, it was essential that the well-being of clients took precedence over the need to secure empirical measures. This meant that treatment needs would always come first and measures would not be collected if they would impact negatively on the progress of treatment or on the mental well-being of a service recipient. Thus, the clinical judgment of the service provider guided data-collection decisions.

Second, non-offending parents were chosen as the key informants of family progress in treatment. Although measures were identified that could be collected from victims and perpetrators, in most instances the cases identified during the term of the project did not proceed far enough into treatment to warrant collection of post-treatment measures from most victimized children and the individuals who sexually assaulted them.

Third, because of the intensity of situations involving child sexual abuse, which is related both to emotional reactivity in parents and to service stress in care providers, it became clear early on that only brief, focused measures could be consistently secured across a wide range of the families being served. Parents coping with personal and family upheaval could not be expected to complete measures that did not have immediate relevancy to their situation. Treatment providers who were heavily taxed with service demands would not employ measures they felt were inappropriate to their clients' mental state or irrelevant to the circumstances of the clinical situation they struggled to ameliorate. Because we were dealing for the most part with parents in highly stressed households, we had to be limited in our instrumentation and flexible in data-gathering.

An ecological perspective (Bronfenbrenner 1979) guided our selection of outcome measures. These included measures at child, parent, family, and social network levels. Empirical measures were classified as being of varying levels of usefulness as indictors of service impact consistent with their centrality to the eco-system surrounding each victim. That is, measures of parental mental well-being and social functioning had highest priority and assessments of social network support had least priority. Measures were selected on the basis of (1) their psychometric strength, (2) the availability of norms for the measure and (3) their use in other child sexual abuse projects in Canada and the United States.

Psychological and Social Adjustment Measures

To secure empirical evidence of the impact of services, two key clinical measures were employed on a repeated basis: at the onset of services (Time 1); approximately six to eight weeks later, following crisis counselling with non-offending parents (Time 2); and approximately six to eight months after treatment services had been initiated (Time 3). The two clinical measures were the Impact of the Event Scale (IES) (Horowitz, Wilner, & Alvarez 1979) and the brief version of the Beck Depression Inventory (Beck & Beck 1972). The IES was used to assess the level of post-traumatic stress disorder associated with the sexual abuse. This scale comprises two major sub-scales: Intrusion and Avoidance. It is a brief, fifteen-item measure with strong internal consistency and evidence of predictive validity (Zilberg, Weiss, & Horowitz 1982). Because depression is the most widely occurring psychological response encountered in mental health services, and the level of depressive symptomatology can be measured adequately through short screening scales, the brief version of the Beck Depression Inventory was also employed as an indicator of psychological distress. This thirteen-item scale is highly correlated with the longer, twenty-one-item scale that has been used extensively in clinical research, and which shows close correspondence to in-depth clinical assessments (Beck & Beck 1972).

Six other clinical practice measures were secured at intake. Clinicians were encouraged to apply these on a repeated basis when they felt a measure was appropriate to the client's situation and would not intrude on the progress of their work. The primary intent of these measures was to assess the psychological and situational circumstances of clients in the test and comparison areas at the onset of services. This served a dual function: it provided information on the status of the cases immediately following disclosure; and it assisted in ensuring that the status of clients entering service in test and comparison areas was equivalent. These measures included the brief version of the Family Assessment Measure (FAM), the UCLA Revised Loneliness Scale, a social network/social support assessment form, the brief version of the Marlow-Crowne Social Desirability Scale, the Child Behaviour Checklist (the Achenbach scale), and the Colorado Child Temperament Inventory (CCTI).

The brief version of the Family Assessment Measure (FAM) is a fourteen-item scale created by selecting the two items that were the most highly correlated with each of the full scale's seven factors. The full version of the FAM is a multi-factorial measure of family functioning that has strong psychometric properties and well-established norms based on circumstances in Canadian families (Skinner, Steinhauer, & Santa-Barbara 1983). The brief version offers a global measure of family adjustment with norms for 'normal' and 'clinical' families. The revised version of the UCLA Loneliness Scale is a well-researched measure of the 'subjective experience' of loneliness or social isolation. It is a twenty-item, unidimensional scale with strong psychometric properties (Russell, Peplau, & Cutrona 1980). Since families experiencing child sexual abuse are believed to be highly socially isolated, this was seen as a potentially important variable that might mediate the impact of coordinated services. As well, a measure of 'actual' social support was employed to collect information on network size and dimensionality (i.e., types of social support), which included family, friends, and professional caregivers who family members could turn to for help and who were available to them at the onset of the project.

A brief version of the Marlow-Crowne Social Desirability Scale was also used in this project (Strahan & Gerbasi 1972). This scale assesses the possible intrusion of the response-style bias of social desirability in self-report measures. The short, ten-item version correlates highly with the full, more widely used, twenty-item version and shows a similar level of internal consistency. Because child sexual abuse is a shame-laden circumstance, the possible intrusion of social desirability was monitored in adult clients from both the test and comparison communities.

Two measures were used to assess the psychological status of the children at the time of disclosure. For children four years of age and older, parents were asked to complete the Child Behavior Checklist (Achenbach & McConaughy 1988). This is one of the most well-established measures of child psychological adjustment and psychopathology. In instances in which the victim of sexual abuse was three years of age or younger, the Colorado Child Temperament Inventory (CCTI) was used to assess the social and psychological functioning of the children (Rowe & Plomin 1977). The CCTI is a parental rating instrument that comprises six sub-scales : sociability, emotionality, activity, attention-span/persistence, reaction to food, and soothability.

Several measures were recommended for use by child therapists when treatment with children was conducted. It was felt that these measures should only be used in situations in which they clearly would not be deleterious to the well-being and adjustment of the children. Since most child therapy was initiated later in the term of the project, the preliminary information collected on these measures will not be included in this chapter. Recommended measures were the Child Attitude Toward Father (CAF) Scale and the Child Attitude Toward Mother (CAM) Scale (Hudson 1982); also the Child Depression Inventory (Fauber, Forehand, Long, Burke & Faust 1987).

Qualitative Interviews

Follow-up 'exit' interviews were conducted with workers and clients to explore their perceptions of the effectiveness of treatment and the impact of the project. Twenty-one workers from the various agencies involved in the project participated. The information gathered was summarized and returned to the workers with a list of questions to consider at a project-sponsored staff retreat in January 1991.

Shortly after the interventions linked to Parent Support Services were completed, a consumer-feedback form was given to each parent who had received service, and this was filled out and returned to the project office without personal identification. The format of this form was closely consistent with the Consumer Satisfaction Questionnaire (CSQ-8) prepared by Attkisson & Zwick (1982). Finally, parent interviews were completed some eighteen months after the principal 'service tracking and data-gathering' phase of the project had been completed.

Timing of Collection of Service Impact Information

Within the principal data-gathering phase of the project, a two-stage data-collection strategy was employed to collect service impact measures from parents of sexually abused children.

Stage one involved the collection of data during the early crisis period linked to the disclosure of the abuse. This first phase of data collection was framed as the period during which the parent support services were delivered. Essentially, Parent Support Services created an opportunity for a project staff person to enter the life of the family, build trust in the parents, and assist them in the resolution of the family crisis resulting from the disclosure of sexual abuse. It also created a bridge into the family that allowed for the early collection of research information at the onset of service. The services were delivered, on average, over an eight-week period.

At the termination of service, stage two involved the completion of a second collection of research measures which offered pre-treatment and post-treatment assessments of the period surrounding the crisis of disclosure. This also provided us with a set of measures at the onset of the coordinated treatment approach in the test community and at the onset of regular services in the comparison community. Another set of measures was collected at the end of the research project. On average this was ten months after services had been initiated for a victimized child and her or his family. Finally, parents were interviewed approximately eighteen months after the end of the principal data-collection phase of the project, to assess long-term effects and satisfaction with early investigation and treatment services.

Securing Informed Consent for Data Collection

Over the one-year term of the project, during which service impact measures were collected, there was a total of seventy disclosures of intrafamilial or trusted-third-party sexual abuse in the two study communities that proceeded to formal investigation. Of these, forty-six families (66 per cent) agreed to participate in the research project and completed written, informed consents. At Time 1 (or T1) – onset of investigative services and parent support services – parents from 34 families (74 per cent of eligibles) completed pre-treatment measures. At Time 2 (or T2) – termination of parent support services – parents from twenty-nine families (63 per cent of eligibles) completed 'early' post-treatment measures. At Time 3 (or T3) – completion of the project – parents from twenty-three families (50 per cent of eligibles) completed 'final' post-treatment measures.

Results of Service Impact Measures

Research findings will be presented across the two major phases of data collection. First, we will report the pre-treatment and post-treatment findings linked to parent support services. Because a closely consistent intervention was applied in both study locales during this early treatment phase, families from both test and comparison areas will be merged as one homogeneous group for the analysis of service impact. This will be a T1:T2 comparison. Then, a review will be made of the service impact on families at the onset and termination of services, comparing the test and comparison areas to explore differences that emerged as a result of the coordinated service approach. This will be a T1:T3 comparison. Finally, we will review T1:T2:T3 findings for key research indicators of service impact.

Parent Support Services: Early Crisis Intervention

A special crisis service (as described in Chapter 5) was created to help bridge the investigation procedures and treatment services required when intrafamilial and trusted-third-party disclosures were received by child welfare authorities. Parent Support Services essentially employed a 'neutral' counsellor, the parent support worker

(PSW), who was not directly responsible to either the police or to child welfare authorities. A primary objective of the service was to enlist the assistance of family members, in particular non-offending parents, to help cope with the immediate crisis that challenged the stability of the family unit. Thus, as quickly as possible after a disclosure of child sexual abuse by the father or step-father, an appointment was made to do individual counselling with the mother. In cases of sibling incest or assault by a trusted third party or extended family members, both mothers and fathers were offered service. Careful attention was given to ensure that similar staff resources were assigned to each of the two study locations, with consistent patterns of intervention over an identical time period. Each of the two sites had its own, separately maintained child welfare agency, police detachments, medical services, and courts. Each site was assigned one formal parent support worker and one worker who was retained as a backup worker to both sites at times of case overload. The workers all had a bachelor's degree in social work and were experienced in providing psychological counselling in situations of social stress. For the most part, clinical supervision was provided by one senior family therapist with extensive experience in community mental health services.

To secure empirical evidence of the impact of the parent support services, two key clinical measures were completed during the first several contacts with non-offending parents, and then at the termination of the crisis services: the Impact of the Event Scale (IES) and the brief version of the Beck Depression Inventory (BDI-BF). For the most part these services were initiated close to the time of the disclosure of the child sexual abuse and were delivered over a six to eight-week period involving one to two hours of client contact per week. As well, shortly after the interventions within Parent Support Services were completed, a consumer feedback form was given to each parent who had received service. As well, approximately one year after receiving service, all parents were contacted by telephone to survey their satisfaction with the parent support services they had received.

Consenting and Non-Consenting Cases in the Parent Support Services

When analysis of the aggregated service information was done, comparing those who took part in the parent support services with those who did not, few differences were found that might suggest bias in the study sample. Of those giving consent to participate in the research project, nine parents did not continue to receive services after brief initial contacts to explain their purpose and to collect pre-treatment information. These parents did not view themselves as being in crisis or needing assistance to cope with the disclosure. This yielded a test cohort of twenty-nine families who initiated and participated in the parent support service.

Impact of Parent Support Services

Depressive symptomatology as measured by the brief form of the Beck Depression Inventory was seen as a key indicator of the psychological well-being of non-offending mothers before and after short-term crisis services. Parents entering parent support services showed a pre-treatment depression level in the moderate range of psychopathology and a post-treatment level in the mild range. This change in level of depression was statistically significant. There were substantially fewer fathers (a total of ten) seen as non-offending parents in the project. Levels of depression in the fathers similarly shifted from the moderate range to the mild range following services. However, these differences did not quite reach statistical significance which, given the size of the score differences, may have been due in part to the small sample size. Levels of depression of non-offending mothers and fathers at the onset of services was not found to be statistically different.

To monitor reduction of post-traumatic stress, scores were compared before and after treatment on the total IES scale and its intrusiveness and avoidance sub-scales. There was a significant difference on the IES total score in the level of mothers' pre-treatment scores and post-treatment scores. When compared to clinical norms for the total IES, the mothers showed pre-treatment levels that were not significantly different than patients requiring brief psychotherapy for traumatic stress disorder. Further, the post-treatment scores following the parent support services were no different than the clinical norms for patients who had received brief psychotherapy for traumatic stress disorder (Horowitz, Wilner, & Alvarez 1979). Although mothers' mean scores on the Avoidance sub-scale of the IES showed improvement between pre-treatment and post-treatment testing, this difference was not quite large enough to reach statistical significance. The mean score differences on the Intrusiveness sub-scale of the IES, which showed improvement between pretreatment and post-treatment, was statistically significant.

Kazdin and Wilson (1978) have cautioned researchers and clinicians about depending solely on averaged scores to assess the impact of clinical services. Averaged scores can be misleading in that they may not adequately reflect the proportions of cases that improve, stay the same, or do worse. As a clinical evaluation procedure, we did a comprehensive clinical post-mortem on those cases that showed no change in psychological functioning or appeared to have deteriorated during the crisis service period.

Six cases were found to involve parents showing low levels of depression at both the onset and end of services. Five of these cases involved alleged assaults by perpetrators who were not members of the nuclear family and one case involved an unsubstantiated disclosure of exhibitionism by the father. In all these situations the parents responded well in supporting the victim, and were in turn supported by other members of the family. Most cases required only minimal intervention by the parent support workers.

Two cases showed no change in the IES scores between the onset and end of services. In both of these instances the IES showed normal levels of stress, and both cases involved particulars in which the parents would not be expected to show stress. In one situation, the allegation involved disclosure of an event that had been resolved three years earlier when a father had been investigated for abusing his wife and children. The father was no longer involved with the family and many of the previous crisis elements had been resolved. The other case involved a female babysitter attempting to have intercourse with a young boy some two-and-a-half years prior to the disclosure. This also did not constitute a crisis in the mind of the single-parent mother of the boy.

There were three cases in which the IES remained high and three cases in which the IES increased during treatment. All six cases involved situations in which husbands or sons were the alleged perpetrators of sexual abuse. Most involved extremely deviant behaviours such as violent physical abuse and, in several instances, bestiality. The mothers in these situations all were highly stressed and faced unresolved family situations at the end of the brief crisis services. These cases will require continued crisis support for the non-offending parents and long term therapy for all family members. Finally, two cases were found to have reduced IES scores but increased levels of depression. In both cases the service had assisted in the resolution of the crisis surrounding disclosure and also brought the parents to an awareness of their social isolation and family difficulties. The resolution of these issues was beyond the scope of brief crisis services.

In no instances did the clinical review of changes at the individual case level indicate that the project had not been helpful to families that predictably would have responded with improved psychological functioning if the services were delivered effectively.

Two consumer feedback surveys were completed. The CSQ-8 was given to parents when the parent support services had ended and parents anonymously sent the completed forms by mail to the research office. Approximately half of the eligible cohort of parents responded. The responses indicated a high level of satisfaction with the parent support services. All respondents indicated that the service helped them deal more effectively with their problems. Three-quarters (73 per cent) of the respondents felt they had received the kind of services they wanted, and most (80 per cent) were satisfied with the service that had been provided. Then, long term follow-up was completed through telephone contact with parents by an independent interviewer approximately eighteen months after they had received parent support services. Twenty-one parents, 72 per cent of those who had received the services, were located and agreed to be interviewed. Every parent responded that, in retrospect, they believed they had a positive relationship with their parent support worker and were very satisfied with the services they had received.

Coordinated Treatment Services: A Comparison of Study Sites

Depressive symptomatology in non-offending parents as measured by the brief form of the Beck Depression Inventory was collected at the onset of services following a disclosure of child sexual abuse (Time 1). A final set of measures was collected within eight to ten months after initiation of services (Time 3). The average time period over which case progress was monitored was ten months. Mothers of abused children in the test site showed a pre-treatment depression level in the moderate range of psychopathology and a post-treatment level in the mild range. This change in level of depression was statistically significant. Mothers in the comparison site showed a pre-treatment level of depression in the moderate range and a post-treatment level in the moderate range. The slight changes in the level of depression in parents in the comparison group were not statistically significant.

In terms of the clinical meaning (or substantive significance) of these measures, it appeared that parents in the comparison community were no different in their level of depressive symptomatology when measured at pre-treatment and at post-treatment. As well, at Time 1 both comparison and test groups were not significantly different for level of depressive symptoms in non-offending parents.

The test group showed significant *substantive* change at Time 3 shifting to the none or minimal range while the comparison group remained at the moderate range. The degree of difference in this change at Time 3 between the comparison group and the test group was not quite large enough to reach *statistical* significance. When one employs statistical tests with small samples, a sizeable difference needs to be achieved in averaged scores when groups are compared. Indeed, given the size of the actual differences in depression scores, this failure to reach statistical significance was likely due in part to the small sample size of the comparative groups at Time 3.

To monitor reduction of post-traumatic stress, scores were compared across test and comparison sites, before and after treatment (Time 1:Time 3) on the total IES score and its Intrusion and Avoidance sub-scales. Overall the total IES scores showed improvement in both test and comparison sites that was statistically significant. When compared to clinical norms for the total IES, the mothers in both test and comparison sites showed pre-treatment levels (Time 1) that were not significantly different than patients in the normative sample who required brief psychotherapy for traumatic stress disorder. Further, the post-treatment scores (Time 3) in both sites were not statistically different than the normative average for patients who had completed brief psychotherapy for traumatic stress disorder.

When Intrusion and Avoidance scores were considered separately, it was found that slightly larger changes had occurred in the reduction of *intrusive experiences* (in which clients found that they could not help thinking or having feelings about the crisis event) than in *avoidance experiences* (in which clients directly avoided talking about the sexual abuse situation or dealing directly with it). In both comparative groups, clients reported at Time 3 that thoughts about the abuse did not disrupt thinking or functioning as severely as they did at the time of disclosure (Time 1). In the test site, the mean of the Intrusion score was markedly reduced. In the comparison site, the mean of the Intrusion score was somewhat reduced. The change in the Intrusion score between Time 1 and Time 3 was found to be statistically significant in the test site but not quite large enough to reach statistical significance in the comparison site. Similarly, clients in the test locale showed a reduction in their Avoidance scores with means showing improved functioning and clients in the comparison locale showed a similar improvement. Statistical tests of difference indicated that these changes were significant in the comparison site but not quite large enough to be statistically significant in the test site. Table 8.1 outlines the mean scores on the IES and its sub-scales in the test and comparison locales as well as for a comparison sample based on prior research norms.

A comprehensive review was completed of those cases that showed deterioration in psychological functioning between Time 2 and Time 3 in both test and comparison sites. It was found that one case out of thirteen (8 per cent) in the test site became worse in terms of the level of depression in the non-offending parent. Analysis of the circumstances of the case revealed that the coordinated approach had not been adequately applied. Although the parent support worker and the child welfare workers had maintained a positive, helpful relationship with the family, the parents felt the police had a negative attitude toward their family and that 'the police were interested only in the law and not people.' It turned out that the officers in question had not been involved in the early phases of the project because their detachment, unlike the others, was not under the direct supervision of the RCMP division collaborating on the project. The detachment had been slow to involve child welfare personnel in the case, which had caused an important disruption in the early investigative process. In the comparison area, three out of ten (30 per cent) cases that were traced from Time 1 to Time 3 showed signs of psychological deterioration in non-offending parents, with heightened depressive symptomatology. It did appear that mean score differences between the control and test groups were shown to be substantively significant when individual case differences were systematically reviewed.

Table 8.1
Comparisons of total IES and sub-scale means: Test area, comparison area and normative scores
(Mean and Standard Deviation scores)

Brief therapy normative cohort (Horowitz, Wilner, and Alvarez 1979)

	Pre-brief therapy	Post-brief therapy
Intrusion	23.1 (9.4)	13.9 (10.9)
Avoidance	20.6 (11.0)	10.5 (10.3)
Total scale	43.7 (17.2)	24.3 (17.8)
	N = 32	N = 32

Test-site cohort (with coordinated services)

	T1	T2	T3
Intrusion	19.6 (6.0)	14.9 (8.5)	13.2 (5.7)
Avoidance	19.6 (5.3)	16.3 (9.7)	15.5 (6.8)
Total scale	39.2 (10.0)	31.1 (17.7)	28.7 (12.2)
	N = 20	N = 8	N = 13

Comparison-site cohort (without coordinated services)

	T1	T2	T3
Intrusion	20.7 (4.1)	16.5 (5.7)	16.1 (5.2)
Avoidance	20.7 (5.7)	18.8 (7.8)	17.1 (5.5)
Total scale	41.4 (8.1)	35.4 (11.5)	33.2 (7.8)
	N = 16	N = 11	N = 10

The overall evidence supported our contention that coordinated service delivery results in improved psychological functioning in non-offending parents, while services based on independent agency functioning results in parents suffering continued psychological distress.

Tracing Changes from Time 1 to Time 2 to Time 3

When elements of post-traumatic stress disorder were considered at Time 1, the Intrusion sub-scale of the IES showed that test families were experiencing a similar level of cognitive disruption in both test and comparison cohorts, as were normative test clients who were in crisis. At Time 2, or immediately after brief crisis coun-

Figure 8.1
Intrusiveness sub-scale of IES:
Test and comparison sites by time interval

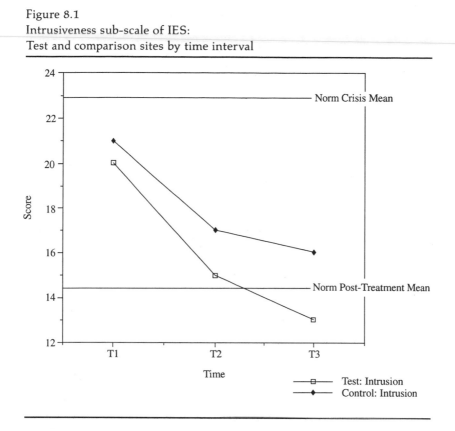

selling, both study cohorts showed scores that were similar to those in normative study clients who had received brief psychotherapy. At Time 3 both comparative groups continued to show decline in the level of their Intrusion scores. The test group showed a steeper decline in their Intrusion scores from Time 2 to Time 3, but these differences were not great enough to be statistically significant. Changes in the Intrusion sub-scale are shown in Figure 8.1.

The tendency to avoid thinking about or dealing with issues relating to sexual abuse seemed to be similarly affected in both the test and comparison groups. At Time 1, which was close to the time of disclosure, both groups showed scores that were closely consistent with a clinical sample of patients with post-traumatic stress disorder. Both groups showed similar improvement at Time

Figure 8.2
Avoidance sub-scale of IES:
Test and comparison sites by time interval

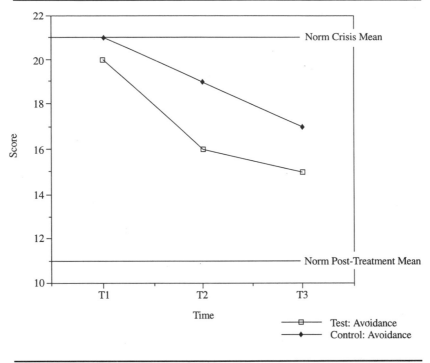

2 and Time 3. Although the test group showed a high rate of improvement at Time 2 and Time 3, these differences were not large enough to reach statistical significance. Both groups appeared to employ avoidance behaviours that could be described as still reflecting vestiges of a post-traumatic stress reaction at Time 3. Changes in the Avoidance sub-scale are shown in Figure 8.2.

Interesting differences were found when the comparison and test groups were compared on the level of depressive symptomatology. Both groups showed levels of depression in the moderate range at the onset of services, which is clinically significant. The comparison group dropped to the mild range and the test group dropped to the mild range immediately following crisis-counselling services. However, at the end of the service tracking period it could be noted

Figure 8.3
Brief Beck depression scale:
Test and comparison sites by time interval

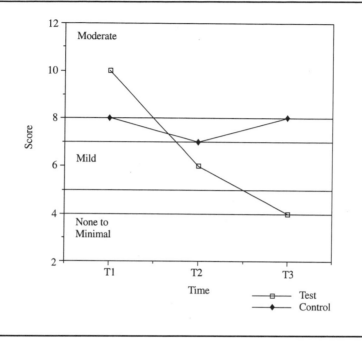

that the comparison group had regressed, showing more depressive symptoms that were on the border of the moderate range, while the test group continued to show a reduction in symptoms of depression reaching the none or minimal category of symptoms of depression. Although the differences between the two groups at Time 3 was of substantive or clinical significance, it was not quite large enough to be statistically significant. Changes in the brief form of the Beck Depression Inventory are shown in Figure 8.3.

Results of the Post-Treatment Follow-Up Interviews with Parents

At the end of the term of the research project, arrangements were made for a neutral person, one who had not been involved in the investigative process, to interview non-offending parents. The purpose was to obtain parents' perceptions of how the service response had been for them and their family members. A standardized interview protocol was employed.

A review was completed of research families who were involved in follow-up interviews and those who were not, to explore possible bias in the sample of respondents. No differences were found that were statistically significant for (1) key perpetrator characteristics (age or type of perpetrator, such as sibling, father, or trusted third party); (2) key victim characteristics (age of victim, degree of sexual intrusion, age at onset of abuse, or duration of abuse situation); or (3) key non-offending parent characteristics (level of traumatic stress reaction, depression, loneliness, or social desirability).

There were two parent characteristics that were not large enough in difference, when respondents and non-respondents were compared, to reach statistical significance, though they did seem clinically significant. These were the measures of depression and family distress collected at the time services were initiated. The non-respondents appeared to be those who were somewhat less depressed and showed less family distress (although neither of these differences was large enough to be statistically significant). Therefore, if there was a bias in the follow-up sample of respondents, it would likely be linked to the inability to secure final research interviews with families experiencing situations that were less troubling to the families and the victims.

Service recipients in the coordinated treatment area did report higher levels of satisfaction in their contacts with child welfare personnel. Although there was a substantial difference in the levels of reported satisfaction with the police in the two comparative areas, this difference was not quite large enough to reach statistical significance. Clients in the coordinated service area appeared to have received more counselling services after disclosure and had higher levels of treatment resources, particularly in terms of child treatment groups, individual counselling for perpetrators, and group treatment for juvenile perpetrators. Highlights of the follow-up interview findings are listed in Table 8.2.

Interpreting Outcome Indicators

The empirical indicators of service impact consistently indicated that the initial crisis resources offered by Parent Support Services was

Table 8.2
Findings of post-treatment interviews with non-offending parents
(N = 26)

Satisfaction with services:			
Overall relationship with CFS			
Test: Good or very good:	88%		
Comparison: Good or very good:	56%		
Satisfaction with police			
Test: Satisfied or very satisfied:	83%		
Comparison: Satisfied or very satisfied:	63%		

Access to services:			
Did any members of your family receive therapy or counselling services that were linked with the sexual abuse situation (after disclosure)?			
Test:	71%	*Comparison*:	29%
Differences found in:			
Access to child treatment group			
Test:	86%	*Comparison*:	14%
Access to perpetrator – individual treatment			
Test:	85% (11/13)	*Comparison*:	43% (3/7)
Access to juvenile perpetrator – group treatment			
Test:	4 cases out of 4	*Comparison*:	0 cases out of 2

of important benefit to parents coping with a disclosure of intra-familial child sexual abuse. In both test and comparison locales, these services facilitated the parents' adjustment to the crisis and reduced psychological distress in non-offending parents. It was also of key research interest to mark the differences that occurred in the more long-term psychological adjustment of parents following the delivery of coordinated investigative and treatment services. Findings supported the contention that coordinated services do result in more rapid recovery and better psychological functioning in those holding the major parenting duties.

Although only brief and focused measures could be employed, these measures did provide evidence that the cases in the test area reported better functioning than those in the comparison area. Parents in the test area reported significantly fewer symptoms of depression following coordinated services, and showed marked reduction in the level to which thoughts about the abuse disrupted their cognitive functioning. Parents in the comparison and test groups both showed a reduction in their tendency to avoid dealing with aspects of the abuse situation, but both groups still had to change substantially in order to bring this avoidance closer to what would be seen clinically as 'normal' levels of avoidance behaviour. Perhaps the term of treatment services available to families in the project was not long enough to deal adequately with the causes of these avoidance patterns.

In studies such as this one, the complex nature of the research question, coupled with the difficulty in securing samples that are adequately large to support statistical analysis procedures, create a substantial challenge in research design. Many of the 'effect sizes' that are associated with key independent variables will be assessed conservatively, because quite large differences will be required to reach statistical significance. It was important in this consideration of service outcomes to consider the clinical or substantive meaning of differences in psychosocial scales, and to complete case-by-case analyses to track positive, neutral, and negative parental responses. Such qualitative analyses provided further evidence that cases did show more improvement in the coordinated service area.

One important challenge to the internal validity of a research design is the potential intrusion of the 'regression effect' (Cook & Campbell 1979). This effect relates to the tendency of extreme scores to move towards the mean through statistical moderation over time. What this means to the clinical evaluator is that cases showing highly deviant scores will tend to improve through a statistical artifact effect rather than being directly and solely an effect of treatment. In studies such as this one, one must be vigilant for such influences on post-treatment scores.

There were indications that regression effects were not distorting the findings of this project. First, the high levels of depression in study subjects did improve following short-term crisis treatment as was anticipated. However, it was also as an important finding that these depression scores did return to a high level for the control subjects but continued to decline to none or minimal signs of depression in the test group. Further, when case-by-case analyses were completed, it did appear that those families that did show improvement were those that clinicians in the test area would affirm were experiencing less psychological stress. Further, those that did not show improvement were those that, according to clinicians, had good reason to continue to be depressed. This served to validate the findings of the psychosocial measures, and did serve as a check for the possible intrusion of regression effects.

It needs to be stressed that only brief and focused measures could be employed in such a highly charged service situation, one that was challenging and stressful for both professional caregivers and service recipients. These modest measures cannot, in and of themselves, establish conclusively that the coordinated service approach was superior to the traditional service approach (i.e., the approach in which each service agency functions separately to meet its independent mandate in ameliorating the circumstances of child sexual abuse). However, the indicators of parental functioning that were employed, and that serve as a means of tracking the overall well-being of the family unit, consistently support the contention that coordinated services do lead to more positive results. In other words, it appears that coordinated investigation and early treatment services do help families recover more quickly from the trauma associated with child sexual abuse.

PART THREE

Reflecting on the Community Experience

9

Professional Attitudes Relating to Child Sexual Abuse

A disclosure of child sexual abuse should trigger a coordinated, interdisciplinary service response. Because a child has been abused and is at risk, child welfare personnel are mandated to investigate. Because a crime has been committed, the criminal justice system must respond. Often the situation will require medical intervention, as an aspect of the investigative and treatment needs of the case and mental health practitioners will often be involved as well to help individuals deal with the crisis of the disclosure and perhaps the long-term psychological effects. In many situations of child sexual abuse, other important social institutions in the life of abused children and their family, such as church and school, may become important actors in the detection and amelioration of the abuse situation.

It is clear that the investigation and treatment of child sexual abuse requires significant effort from a number of human service agencies. However, in most locales these basic services remain fragmented and characterized by interdisciplinary distrust and independent action (Finkelhor 1984).

In a survey of professionals from a number of the key disciplines involved in services to sexually abused children and their families, Finkelhor (1984) found that there was a differential use of interprofessional consultation by different service sectors. Child welfare workers tended to use as wide a range of resources (e.g., medical, mental health, school) as they could in investigating the disclosure of abuse, to reduce its long-term impact on the child and the family.

School personnel and mental health practitioners were less open to engage with other professionals. This was viewed as being due in part to the focused responsibility these services see themselves holding with respect to serving children, and because of the tradition of information-confidentiality maintained by school and mental health personnel. Criminal justice services were found to be the service sector with the least bridging to other professional groups.

Key to this pattern of isolated action by different professional groups was the difference in their views regarding the meaning of child sexual abuse, and the implications this has for beliefs about strategies of intervention to curb and manage it (MacFarlane & Bulkley 1982). Saunders (1988) found important differences in attitudes when child welfare and criminal justice personnel were compared. A key philosophical difference was found in the 'retribution – rehabilitation debate,' in which police officers and judges were more prone to taking a punitive stance than child welfare workers. Similarly, Kelley (1990) provides evidence that police officers recommend more severe punishment for offenders than social workers or nurses. Wilk and McCarthy (1986), in one of the few studies involving professionals from rural settings, suggest that police officers are more hard line than child welfare or mental health workers. When comparing child protective social workers and attorneys, Craft and Clarkson (1985) found differences in support for court action. Social workers recommended court action less frequently, a difference that seemed related to physical injury of the child, previous family history of abuse, parental reaction, and parental admission of involvement.

Attias and Goodwin (1985) found that gender may play a more important role in professional response to child sexual abuse than professional affiliation. Males tended to overestimate the proportion of false allegations made by children, to underestimate the prevalence of father-daughter incest, and to fail to act when children appeared to retract their allegations of sexual assault.

Difference in philosophy between members of major professional groups involved in investigation and treatment was of key research interest in this project. We planned a two-stage process to study ideological differences in professionals. First, we wished to explore the possibility of developing an empirical measure that could tap essential aspects of professional attitudes with regard to intervention. It was our intent to widely survey police officers, child welfare workers, and community mental health staff as central actors in the investigation and management of child sexual abuse cases in the project area. It was our hope to construct a measure of professional ideology. As a second step, we wished to explore the impact that the development of coordinated services might have on professional attitudes, using the developed empirical measure as a major dependent variable. It was of research interest to explore whether the coordinated treatment approach resulted in more consistent views across professional groups participating in investigation and treatment activities. Because of the importance of the professional view of gender with regard to the seriousness of the abuse and the need for intervention, it was our intent to explore the attitudes within the major service sectors while controlling for gender differences.

Developing the Professional Attitude Scale

Three key professional groups were surveyed in both test and comparison communities: police, child welfare workers, and community mental health staff. Our pool of professional respondents was expanded to include all police child welfare, and mental health staff in the geographic regions immediately surrounding the research communities. This would generate a large enough sample size (for the multivariate analyses required in scale building) and would ensure that we were using a pool of homogeneous professionals from which sub-samples of key service sectors could be drawn for more focused analysis of changes in professional attitude.

Each key service sector was approached through the formal channels that existed in the study locale. This process involved an initial contact by letter to local service authorities to explain the rationale for the project and to gain permission to involve field staff. Each service group independently sanctioned the research and facilitated the involvement of field staff. All professional respondents had the option of identifying themselves or completing their survey forms anonymously. All staff members of the child welfare and community mental health agencies agreed to participate and completed all research measures. This resulted in a final sample of thirty-five child welfare workers and twenty-one community mental health practitioners. A sampling frame was created listing all police officers serving the geographic area included in this study. Attitudinal measures were dispatched from each police station to 122 officers. Completed measures were received from 80 officers, yielding a final response rate of 66 per cent. The research questionnaires comprised items relating to the social demographics and work histories in child sexual abuse of each respondent as well as a collection of twenty-two likert-type attitudinal items relating to the causes of child sexual abuse and to intervention preferences.

Creating a Child Sexual Abuse Scale to Assess Professional Beliefs

A Professional Attitudes Regarding the Sexual Abuse of Children (PARSAC) scale was constructed to include sixteen items combining to form three main factors or attitude domains:

1. *Beliefs with Regard to Extensiveness and Seriousness of the Issue*

   This item assessed the tendency of a professional to see child sexual abuse as a widespread occurrence in the community and of important psychological impact on victims, rather than a phenomenon that was rare and not necessarily psychologically damaging to children.

2. *Treatment Versus Punishment Priority*

   This item related to the philosophical stance taken with regard to whether priority is placed on punishment or on treatment as the most important or preferred intervention. It touched on the debate in the field as to what priority should be given to bringing criminal charges against the abuser, and the use of incarceration as an important deterrent to child sexual abuse.

3. *View Regarding Identity of Those Who Perpetrate Child Sexual Abuse*

   This item focused on a professional's recognition that a wide range of individuals perpetrate sexual abuse against children and that offenders are not necessarily members of deviant groups in society.

The empirical properties of the PARSAC scale (including the specifics of the varimax factor solution), the items contained in the scale, and statistical analyses relating to interprofessional differences are available elsewhere for interested researchers and clinicians (Trute, Adkins, & MacDonald 1992).

Statistical analyses were performed on the total PARSAC scale and its three sub-scale scores, comparing the three professional groups included in the study (police, child welfare, community mental health). On the total PARSAC score, police officers had a significantly lower total score than child welfare and community mental health workers. When these difference in professional view were more closely explored across each of the three factors in the scale, police officers remained the lowest scoring professional group. On factor one (the view regarding the seriousness of the issue), police officers scored significantly lower than child welfare workers. This would suggest that police officers and child welfare workers differ in their view of how extensive such abuse is in the community and the serious impact such acts have on victims. On factor two (treatment vs. punishment priority) police officers scored significantly lower than both child welfare and community mental health personnel. This suggested that police officers tended to view treatment as less effective, and to a stance that placed greater emphasis on punishment. On factor three (perpetrator identity) police officers scored significantly lower than child welfare workers. That is, it indicated that child welfare workers were more likely than police to acknowledge that child sexual abuse occurred in many different types of families and was instigated by many different types of perpetrators.

When gender differences in attitudes relating to child sexual abuse were tested on the PARSAC total and sub-scale scores, women were found to have significantly higher scores on the total scale and on each of the three sub-scale scores. When statistical tests were performed that controlled for gender while comparing professional differences, gender was found to be a significant influence. As well, statistically significant differences remained between professional groups for scores on the total scale and for two of the sub-scales: 'treatment vs. punishment priority' and 'perpetrator identity.' However, one of the sub-scales, 'seriousness of issue,' showed no difference between groups when the analysis was controlled for gender. Table 9.1 shows mean scores adjusted for gender for each professional group.

Table 9.1
Comparison of mean scores: PARSAC scale adjusted for gender of professional

	Child Welfare	Community Mental Health	Police
Total Mean Score**	51.68	49.99	45.90
Factor 1: Seriousness of issue	20.67	20.39	19.51
Factor 2: Treatment/Punishment**	14.98	14.35	11.77
Factor 3: Perpetrator Identity*	16.01	15.24	14.61

Significant differences: ** $p < .001$ * $p < .01$

Assessing Changes in Professional Attitudes During the Early Development of the Coordinated Service Approach

It was of research interest to note if the implementation of the coordinated treatment approach had served to immediately alter professional attitudes towards child sexual abuse; that is, if any change had occurred over time in the total PARSAC score. The 'treatment vs. punishment' sub-scale of the PARSAC was of particular interest because this sub-scale appeared to tap the most contentious aspect of interdisciplinary practice.

Professionals were assessed separately in both test and comparison communities at the onset of the project (Time 1), one year after the coordinated approach had been initiated (Time 2), and two years after (Time 3). The groups studied included members of the coordinated treatment team[1] in the test area; also child welfare personnel, community mental health staff, and police officers in the test and comparison areas.

We wished to consider separately whether the coordinated service approach served to alter professional attitudes in those human service professionals who were most closely involved in interdisciplinary

[1] The coordinated treatment team comprised staff from child welfare, community mental health, probation, mental retardation services, and a women's shelter.

treatment. Twenty-six professionals had been involved in the coordinated treatment team during the research period and twenty-one of these completed attitudinal measures that tracked scores over time.

Because the child welfare agency served as the central hub of the coordinated system, it was of interest to assess whether any change had occurred in the members of the CFS 'south team' in both the test and comparison areas. Members of this team in each of the comparative sites had been directly involved in the investigative and early treatment services that had been monitored during the course of this project. Nine child welfare social workers, out of a potential of nine, completed attitudinal measures over the term of the project from the test community. Six child welfare social workers, out of a potential of nine, completed measures in the comparison community.

Community mental health staff from government services and from a local mental health centre played an important part in the treatment process. Analysis was done of all community mental health personnel who served both adults and children in the geographic locales included in this project. This included twelve of a possible fifteen staff from the test site, and eleven of a possible thirteen staff from the comparison site.

Finally, attention was given to the impact that the coordinated approach may have had on police officers serving in the test and comparison communities. Sampling police officers was a difficult task. It required a multi-stage distribution of questionnaires that involved preliminary approval from senior staff, coordination of questionnaire distribution through staff sergeants at individual detachments, and anonymous mail return by individual police officers.

A major problem encountered in the long-term tracking of police attitudes was the rotation of officers – not a trivial matter, as there were large numbers of police officers transferred over limited time periods. At the onset of the project there were 122 officers serving in the two research locales. After a two-year period, only 27 officers remained from the original cohort of 122 that had lived for at least a two-year period in the study community and had had any experience in child sexual abuse matters.

Because of the difficulty in completing police surveys, a two-stage strategy for data gathering was followed. First, all police officers were surveyed at Time 1 and Time 3. Then, analysis was completed of a subset of the officers at Time 3. This subset included the twenty-seven officers that had been in the study communities throughout. This final subset included thirteen out of a possible eighteen officers from the test area and seven out of a possible nine officers in the comparison site.

Therefore, to track professional attitudes over time, we followed four cohorts of professionals over a two-year period: fifteen child welfare staff, twenty-three community mental health staff, twenty police officers, and twenty-one members of the coordinated treatment team in the test community.

The Coordinated Treatment Team

The bulk (91 per cent) of the members of the coordinated treatment team were between the ages of twenty-six and thirty-five (33 per cent) or thirty-six and forty-five (57 per cent). Almost two-thirds (62 per cent) were female. Approximately one-quarter (24 per cent) had spent less than five years in their professional role, one-third (33 per cent) for six to ten years and almost half (43 per cent) for over ten years. Of the participants on the coordinated treatment committee almost half (43 per cent) were child welfare staff, one-third (33 per cent) mental health personnel, and almost one-quarter (24 per cent) were from other human service settings such as probation departments or crisis and women's shelters. Approximately two-thirds (62 per cent) of these professionals saw one to ten cases per year and one-fifth (19 per cent) saw twenty-six or more per year.

Treatment team scores on the total PARSAC scale and on the 'treatment vs. punishment' sub-scale remained unchanged at Time 1, Time 2, and Time 3 (see Table 9.2). There were no significant differences between the measures at the three time periods. It should be noted that attitudinal scores were at a high level both at the onset and throughout the course of the project. Participants perceived that child sexual abuse was a serious societal issue, that it occurred in many sectors of the community, and that treatment should be given high priority in these situations. It was clear that local caregivers shared the view that child sexual abuse services should be given high service priority in their local community, and they were prepared to commit significant time and effort to create a coordinated community service response. Without this positive

Table 9.2
Attitudes towards child sexual abuse: Views of members of the coordinated
treatment team at three time intervals

	Total PARSAC score		Treatment/punishment sub-scale	
	Mean	(SD)	Mean	(SD)
T1	48.3	(3.8)	15.1	(2.5)
T2	48.5	(3.9)	15.2	(1.9)
T3	48.1	(5.5)	15.0	(2.5)

attitude, shared beliefs, and enduring commitment to treatment, it is unlikely that a coordinated service system could have been as readily initiated and maintained as it was in this case study.

The Child Welfare Staff

The bulk (93 per cent) of the child welfare staff that were tracked over time were between the ages of twenty-six and thirty-five (33 per cent) or thirty-six and forty-five (60 per cent). Approximately half (53 per cent) were female. Approximately one-quarter (27 per cent) had spent less than five years in their professional role, one-quarter (27 per cent) had been in this role for six to ten years, and almost half (47 per cent) had been working in their professional capacity for eleven years or more. Approximately one-third (33 per cent) of these professionals saw one to ten cases per year and two-fifths (40 per cent) saw twenty-six or more cases per year. A statistical comparison of the test and comparison areas indicated that there were no significant differences in child welfare staff in the two sites for age, sex, years of work experience, or size of child sexual abuse caseload.

Child welfare staff total PARSAC scores, and scores on the 'treatment vs. punishment' sub-scale, remained unchanged in the test and comparison groups of child welfare workers at Time 1, Time 2, and Time 3 (see Table 9.3).

At the onset of the project there were significant differences in measured attitudes in child welfare staff from the test and comparison communities. Those in the test area had higher scores on the 'treatment vs. punishment' sub-scale than child welfare person-

Table 9.3
Attitudes towards child sexual abuse: Views of child welfare staff in test and
comparison communities at three time intervals

| | Total PARSAC score | | | | Treatment/Punishment Sub-scale | | | |
	Test		Comparison		Test		Comparison	
T1	49.0	(4.1)	44.6	(2.1)	15.9	(2.4)	12.8	(3.0)
T2	49.0	(4.7)	45.5	(2.1)	16.3	(1.8)	13.6	(1.8)
T3	49.4	(5.8)	46.7	(2.9)	15.8	(2.1)	13.8	(1.8)

nel from the comparison area, a difference that bordered on statistical significance. They began the project with a higher level of belief in the utility of coordinated treatment approaches and a lesser regard for punishment as a deterrent to child sexual abuse. As the project progressed, the child welfare staff in the comparison area showed more treatment-oriented beliefs and, throughout the course of the project approached the score maintained by the child welfare staff in the test site.

Although the child welfare personnel in the test area remained significantly different from the police on the 'treatment vs. punishment' sub-scale throughout the project, the child welfare staff in the comparison area showed scores on this attitudinal domain that did not significantly differ from police at Time 3.

Community Mental Health Staff

Mental health professionals being followed over time varied across age ranges. Approximately one-fifth (22 per cent) were between the ages of twenty-six and thirty-five, two-fifths (39 per cent) between thirty-six and forty-five, one-third (30 per cent) between forty-six and fifty-five years, and one-tenth (9 per cent) were over fifty-five. Approximately two-fifths (44 per cent) were female. Approximately one-tenth (9 per cent) had spent less than five years in their professional role, one-quarter (26 per cent) had been in this role for six to ten years, and three-fifths (65 per cent) had served in this role for eleven years or more. Approximately two-thirds (71 per cent) of these professionals saw one to ten cases per year and about one-tenth (14 per cent) saw eleven or more. A statistical comparison of test and comparison areas indicated no significant differences

Table 9.4
Attitudes towards child sexual abuse: Views of mental health staff in test and
comparison communities at three time intervals

	Total PARSAC score				Treatment/Punishment Sub-scale			
	Test		Comparison		Test		Comparison	
T1	44.6	(3.4)	48.3	(2.3)	14.1	(2.3)	14.6	(1.9)
T2	45.9	(3.3)	47.9	(3.3)	14.6	(1.0)	14.3	(1.5)
T3	46.0	(3.9)	47.2	(3.9)	14.4	(1.4)	13.6	(2.0)

in community mental health staff in the two sites for age, sex, years
of work experience, or size of child sexual abuse caseload.

Community mental health total PARSAC scores and scores on
the 'treatment vs. punishment' sub-scale remained unchanged at
Time 1, Time 2, and Time 3 (see Table 9.4).

Police Officers

Police officers varied in age. One-tenth (10 per cent) were under
twenty-five years of age, one-quarter (25 per cent) were between
twenty-six and thirty-five, half (50 per cent) were between thirty-
six and forty-five, and more than one-tenth (15 per cent) between
forty-six and fifty-five. A small proportion, one in ten (10 per cent)
were female. One-quarter (25 per cent) had spent less than five
years in their professional role, 15 per cent had been in this role
for eleven to fifteen years, and three-fifths (60 per cent) had served
for sixteen years or more. Approximately four-fifths (79 per cent)
saw one to ten cases of child sexual abuse per year and about one-
fifth (21 per cent) saw eleven to twenty-five cases per year.

There were no significant differences in police officers in the test
and comparison sites for age or years of work experience. However,
there were significantly more female officers in the comparison area.
It was found that for police officers as a group there were no significant differences between male and female officers on the total
PARSAC scale or on the treatment vs. punishment sub-scale. In
such circumstances it is not clear if women who join the police
force already hold beliefs similar to the men or if the experience
of policing over time leaves female officers with beliefs that are
closely compatible with those held by the male police officers.

Table 9.5
Attitudes towards child sexual abuse: Views of police officers in test and comparison communities in two time intervals

| | Total PARSAC score | | | | Treatment/Punishment Sub-scale | | | |
	Test		Comparison		Test		Comparison	
T1	47.8	(4.3)	47.6	(4.0)	11.9	(2.5)	11.7	(2.3)
T3	41.2	(3.5)	42.3	(6.8)	10.7	(2.8)	11.6	(2.7)

Police total PARSAC scores appeared to be reduced or to reflect more negative attitudes over time in both rural communities. Similarly, scores on the 'treatment vs. punishment' sub-scale appeared to be slightly reduced in both communities for police officers between Time 1 and Time 3. However the degree of these differences was not great enough to be statistically significant (see Table 9.5).

Summary of Findings Relating to the Measurement of Professional Attitudes

When an allegation of child sexual abuse is made, a number of human service agencies will view it as their responsibility to respond, and each will have a particular service interest that will frame their work. However, each will have also a common need to stop the abuse and ameliorate the negative future consequences of the abusive situation. Rather than have a stream of professionals entering the life of the child and family in a random and repetitive manner, it is clearly preferable to implement investigative and treatment services in a planned, thoughtful, and coordinated way.

It seems that a major element in the creation of such coordinated services is the presence of a shared ideology in which professionals hold in common some beliefs about (1) the factors that contribute to the basic causes of child sexual abuse, (2) how sexual abuse can impact on the well-being of a child (and the child's family), and (3) what might be done to reduce the negative consequences of the abusive situation. These attitudinal domains are measured in the PARSAC scale (Trute, Adkins, & MacDonald 1992).

The gender of human service professionals is a strong indicator of attitude towards child sexual abuse. Women were found to have significantly higher scores on all three sub-scales of the PARSAC scale. This is consistent with the findings of Attias and Goodwin (1985). In their survey of psychologists, psychiatrists, pediatricians and family counsellors, it was clear that gender, rather than discipline or personal clinical experience, was the most powerful predictor of attitudes regarding incest. They observed: "More men than women overestimated the percentage of children who make false accusations of sexual abuse. More men than women underestimated the prevalence of father-daughter incest in the general population. More men than women would choose not to report to child protective services a child who had retracted" (p. 532). Concern has been expressed elsewhere about the implications of gender differences with respect to the legal process and the administration of the law in sexual assault cases and incest. Jackson (1985), in a study of the attribution of incest blame among rural attorneys and judges, found marked differences based on the gender of the attorney.

In our study, females scored significantly higher on each of the three sub-scales of the PARSAC Scale. That is, men were less inclined than women to regard the sexual abuse of children as widespread or serious, men were more likely than women to see punishment and retribution as an effective deterrent to the sexual abuse of children, and men were more likely to see perpetrators as individuals who stood out in some way from the general population. Since the bulk of police officers in our study were male and the bulk of the social workers were female, the interdisciplinary differences can in some part be explained by gender differences. However, the question remains as to whether men and women come to these professions with their beliefs ready-made or whether the professional role, over time, does serve to shape the perceptions and beliefs of the men and women who must serve within a specific professional context. Our findings suggest that in any interdisciplinary comparisons of major service providers in situations of child sexual abuse, care must be taken to consider gender effects.

When attitudes were compared across professional groups, our findings corroborated prior research that differentiated police from other human service professionals. We found that police were significantly different on all three sub-scales of the PARSAC scale when compared to child welfare workers and community mental health personnel. However, this difference was moderated when analysis was controlled by gender. After adjusting for gender, it was found that police officers still differed from child welfare workers

with respect to their view that punishment had a priority in curtailing child sexual abuse. As well, they tended to identify perpetrators as coming from deviant sectors of the population. Concerning perception of the seriousness of the issue, differences between
professional groups lost statistical significance when they were adjusted for gender. It was interesting to note that, within the ranks
of the police force, there did not appear to be significant gender
differences in attitudes regarding child sexual abuse. The female
and male police officers appeared to hold beliefs that were closely
similar.

It should be noted that although statistically significant differences were found between the professional groups, the absolute
scores on the attitude sub-scales were close in value. That is, although these differences were great enough not to be caused by
chance factors, they still reflected a similarity of view and were
all at the high end of the scale. Perhaps the most meaningful differences occurred in the 'treatment vs. punishment' dimension. This
was the sub-scale that maintained a distinctive difference between
professional groups even when adjusted for gender of the respondent. One could conclude that in the rural communities involved in
our study, there is a great deal of similarity of view between police,
child welfare agencies and community mental health staff on those
aspects of child sexual abuse relating to misinformation and stereo-
typed perceptions. That is, it seems human service personnel are
more consistently informed about the widespread occurrence of
child sexual abuse, about the serious effect it has on children and
their families, and about the ways in which subtle intrusions (such
as the presence of pornography or acts of fondling) constitute an
abusive sexual assault on a child. Further, the professional groups
appear to be close in their view that many adult members, across
a wide cross-section of the community, may be abusers of children.

The key area of difference between professional groups appears
linked to the issue of what should be done with those who perpetrate
the sexual abuse. This is a perplexing issue that is difficult to resolve
for many professionals across the human services (Finkelhor 1984).
The difference between police and the other human service professionals in the matter of 'retribution versus rehabilitation' is not
surprising. It is generally recognized that police and social workers
approach social problems from different vantage points. Hechler
(1988) has identified this difference as social workers striving to

bring change through strategies of cooperation, while police strive to enforce the law with uncooperative people through confrontation Saunders (1988) has reflected on such differences in basic 'belief systems' between the police and other human service professionals, and has highlighted the need to attend to these issues in coordinating services. Left as they are, the differences in ideology do not augur well for the smooth development of a coordinated approach to sexual abuse investigation and treatment planning. One professional group may push for tight evidence and strong legal intervention to curb sexual abuse; another may push for the overall social, physical, and mental well-being of the child, which would include strengthening the remaining remnants of what was once a family unit.

A serious challenge faces those who wish to advance services in this sensitive and important area. The challenge is to create an interdisciplinary atmosphere where differences in professional values and service approach can be mutually appreciated and respected. This would be a working atmosphere in which each professional group can fulfil its own professional mandate, while finding a course of intervention that cooperates with a coordinated service plan and works in the best interest of the victimized child and his or her family.

10

Conclusions and Recommendations

The investigation and treatment of intrafamilial child sexual abuse is a stressful circumstance for victims and their families, as well as for the professionals who are responsible for intervening in their lives. Most agencies that seek to protect children from sexual abuse, or to deal with the aftermath of a sexual assault on a child, tend to be fragmented in their service delivery and narrow in their scope of services. The field is characterized by an extended investigative response and delayed treatment activities for those who perpetrate and those who suffer. Treatment has tended to focus narrowly on victims or perpetrators while ignoring the fact that there is an entire family system in trouble. There is evidence that the institutional response to child sexual abuse by those mandated to investigate and protect can exacerbate the trauma through repeated questioning of victims, intense intrusion into the lives of family members, and the creation of imminent threats to family composition and stability (Martin 1992). The findings of this rural demonstration project suggest that a coordinated approach to service delivery, one in which agencies collaborate in the investigation and early treatment of child sexual abuse, can be beneficial to child victims and their family members. In a coordinated model of service delivery it appears that more treatment resources can be mobilized, less stressful investigative circumstances can be created, and psychological distress in parents can be more readily eased.

However, the implementation and maintenance of a coordinated service system is not without significant cost in time and energy.

In this project we witnessed an escalating service demand as more cases were identified than had been the norm in the area, and as professionals were called upon to dedicate more time than would usually be allotted to each case. The increased time was linked to the numerous collateral contacts required with the other professionals holding a mutual involvement or service interest in each case. The service pressures on all investigators and treatment providers seemed to rise in intensity as more collaborative effort was required, and as closer collegial scrutiny of service delivery was maintained.

The message that was clearly communicated to us from our study experience is that the coordinated approach is more beneficial, but it is not possible to maintain without some increase in professional services. It was our experience that these increased service costs in response to child sexual abuse can be modest in scope. The increased costs fundamentally involve the creation of several part-time but essential service positions (the service coordinator and parent support worker) and the funding of local professionals for their travel and time while participating in ongoing planning and consultation activities (the community treatment committee).

In this demonstration project, basic service resources were maintained at their usual level in the 'test community' by child welfare agencies, mental health services, and police. This was happening even though the demands for service time were steadily growing as a consequence of the coordinated interagency approach. It was not without a heroic effort that high-quality services could be maintained as demands on professionals' time rose and basic service resources (e.g., number of practitioners, travel budgets, etc.) were not concomitantly increased. It is not reasonable to expect rural communities to implement coordinated services for the investigation and treatment of child abuse without providing additional resources, particularly in service sectors that are mandated to respond to each disclosure of abuse.

This demonstration project served to identify and highlight the essential components of a coordinated treatment model in Canadian rural communities. These included the fundamental need to draw local service agencies together in a shared, collaborative, planning process. The process was based on the premise that coordinated services must be primarily implemented, monitored, and maintained by line-level service providers – the key actors in such integrated systems. However, it was clear that allied commitment needed to be developed as well at senior administrative levels in each of the participating agencies. Administrators could support the efforts of their line staff or sabotage them by tightening resources or limiting participation (e.g., through assigning too-large caseloads or prohibiting the travel required to attend collaborative community planning meetings).

At a higher political level, it is also important to secure support from provincial government departments to ensure that inter-departmental bridging is created which facilitates key policy elements such as investigatory guidelines. Such guidelines should require inter-disciplinary investigation and social-psychological assessments. They should identify child sexual abuse as a high service priority that warrants careful interdepartmental attention. (That is, that child sexual abuse is a legitimate 'mental health issue' deserving of involvement by the Department of Health or is considered a high priority, criminal-justice issue requiring special attention by crown attorneys in the department of Justice.) The design of a coordinated treatment system needs political support most profoundly at the 'grass roots' level. However, this support must be developed at various levels of authority, up to senior provincial departmentals such as (in the case of Manitoba) the departments of Health, Family Services, and Justice.

At the local community level, it seems that three fundamental components need to be created for a coordinated service system: a community treatment committee, a service coordinator and a case manager. First, a community treatment committee needs to be formally structured to provide a forum for community service planning by participating agencies. It is within the scope of the committee to provide opportunities for the sharing and understanding of differing professional ideologies with respect to the handling of child sexual abuse situations. It functions as a vehicle for formal case reviews and the evolution of a service system in which community professionals understand how patterns of collaborative investigation and treatment can be best maintained in their local area. It is a useful structure for the provision of training and supervision in content areas in which there is heightened local need. In retrospect we would suggest that several times each year, formal expanded meetings of the community treatment committee should be held, involving the participation of agency heads and senior management. This might serve to ensure that developments in the field by line-level staff were understood, appreciated, and supported at higher levels of administrative authority in each participating human service agency.

It is vital in a coordinated service system that one person is identified as the local 'traffic cop' for all identified cases of child sexual abuse. This person acts as the service coordinator and has formal responsibility for seeing that there is a planned and smoothly functioning bridge between those who do the investigative work and those who provide treatment services. The service coordinator ensures that the community treatment committee meets regularly, to maintain interagency communication and service collaboration. He or she works to secure a case manager for each treatment situation linked to a sexually abused child and monitors the functioning of each case manager.

Although practice supervision for individual treatment providers is supplied by their home agency according to their discipline's standards and protocols, the case manager must monitor each case to be sure each treatment provider is meeting her or his commitments within a systemic treatment strategy. Although a number of professionals may be involved in the treatment of a family in which there has been child abuse, a chief difficulty in such treatment has been the absence of a central person or agency to help direct the whole process (Baglow 1990). In our model, the case manager serves this function. This means that the case manager ensures that every abused child has a comprehensive treatment plan involving both the child and family members, and that treatment is delivered in a thoughtful, sequential manner that is appropriate to the circumstances of each case.

Each treatment plan is developed as a balance between what a case requires and what resources can be secured in the home community. In our experience it called for local caregivers to try to meet high priority needs with very limited resources. It led to the creation of new, collaboratively-established local treatment resources (e.g., child therapy groups and group therapy for juvenile perpetrators) to maximize the slim treatment resources in the rural communities.

The coordinated approach includes three service phases which are not mutually exclusive and which may overlap sequentially: the disclosure phase, the investigative phase, and the treatment phase. The disclosure phase is that period of time in which the sexual abuse is characterized by the realization that this is a family in which children are not protected (internal threat), and that this is a family that is under investigation (external threat). It was our experience that a parent support worker was a valuable preventative mental health resource during the disclosure phase and that the cost of the service was modest. The parent support worker immediately contacted 'non-offending' parents at the time of the allegation and offered service to assist in the management of all the family issues relating to the disclosure. The parent support worker was not there to judge whether or not child sexual abuse had occurred, but to help a parent cope with the family crisis created by the allegation. We found that this short-term crisis service prevented families from quickly closing ranks and becoming 'emotional fortresses,' fending off all outside professional intruders. We found that the service also helped parents become more sensitive to their child's distress, and helped them give the child more positive support and better protection in their homes. We found that most parents accepted the offer of such services, and that the bulk of those who did use this crisis service greatly appreciated how helpful it had been at a very troubled time in the life of their families.

During the investigative phase evidence was collected concerning whether or not the allegation of child sexual abuse could be substantiated. A critical feature of this phase was the service interface between child welfare and police investigators. In our experience this was the most challenging component of the coordinated model. It was clear that these two professional groups held conflicting intervention ideologies that were linked to their different service mandates. The key aspect of this professional difference seems linked to attitudes regarding the priority of treatment versus punishment in responding to child sexual abuse. The police are responsible for collecting evidence that can lead to criminal convictions for violations of the law. Child welfare workers are primarily concerned about the safety and well-being of children in the context of their social environment. Child welfare investigators seek somewhat different elements of evidence than police, and reach conclusions based on different degrees of proof. However, through formal negotiation and thoughtful planning of collaborative investigative procedures, immediate benefits can be gained for both the criminal justice and child welfare systems and for the children and families they are meant to serve.

The basic service ideologies of these two primary agencies with mandated or legislated responsibilities seem highly resistant to change. Perhaps investigative procedures and protocols need to be altered first, so that they are more sensitive to victims and their families, applied in a more consistent manner, and are more clearly understood and thoughtfully applied by police and child welfare workers. Perhaps similarity in attitudes and interprofessional respect between police officers and child welfare staff will follow.

It is our belief that, in rural Canadian communities, the Royal Canadian Mounted Police should maintain specialized sexual abuse teams rather than relegate this difficult work to the routine duty of each police officer. Currently, if a child sexual abuse disclosure comes to the attention of the police, whoever is on duty at that time pursues the investigation. This may be an officer who has little training, experience, or interest in this area. We would argue that gathering evidence in child sexual abuse cases is a highly specialized situation, and that interagency collaboration is required between police and child welfare authorities. Such collaboration would certainly serve to streamline and enhance communications between child welfare and police investigators in rural communities, and could substantially remedy the now fractious interface between child welfare agencies and the police.

Perhaps one of the most frustrating aspects of planning treatment services in situations of child sexual abuse is the long judicial process, which often delays and disrupts effective intervention, and will often further slow down the initiation of clinical intervention in these cases. Child abuse cases because of their socially complex and emotionally powerful nature, almost always require long-term and intensive treatment services. During the term of this project, some flexibility in court dispositions was secured for juvenile offenders. However, the criminal court did not deviate from its traditional practices with adult perpetrators. This created a major impediment to the delivery of immediate and coordinated treatment services for families in which incest had occurred.

With more time and resources, we would have wished to explore the development of more closely integrated court and treatment functions. The 'Godfather Offer' (MacFarlane & Bulkey 1982) seems a promising option to pursue. This essentially offers an alternative path that avoids criminal prosecution if the defendant acknowledges responsibility for the abuse, makes a commitment to a treatment plan, and agrees to other provisions such as those that relate to the securing of sexual protection and safety in the family. Mac-Farlane and Bulkley identify a number of benefits that such an alternative to sentencing would offer, such as the securing of a guilty plea and avoidance of the delays and expense of litigation and testifying in court, speedier access to treatment services for victim and family members, and avoidance of a prison term and loss of employment for the perpetrator. Although there are both positive and negative aspects to an approach that links court and treatment services it could facilitate more effective interventions in many situations of intrafamilial child sexual abuse.

In some instances, the formal and traditional court procedures will be most appropriate. However, even in these situations, more thoughtful integration of the criminal justice and treatment systems is also needed. Certainly any procedural innovations that can better serve the interests of child victims should be pursued. The innovative court preparation work pioneered in the Province of Ontario by Sas and her associates (1991) deserves more extensive recognition in Canadian courts.

The importance of linking the power of the courts with the process of therapy is well recognized in the child sexual abuse literature. The courts can facilitate compliance to enter treatment and can influence continued participation in therapy. Furniss (1991) clarifies the differences between 'linear' interventions such as court control of perpetrators, and 'systemic' interventions such as family systems treatment. Both are recognized as necessary interventions that can be integrated into a coordinated program of treatment of intrafamilial child sexual abuse. Baglow (1990) similarly considers the 'containment' the courts can provide as a necessary and integral aspect of effective treatment of child abuse.

The interface between investigative and treatment activities is a profound aspect of the planning in a coordinated service system. In our experience, managing this interface was one of the important roles of the service coordinator. It was this person's responsibility to watch the initial progress of the case, maintain contact with investigators and, at the first opportunity, bridge to the case managers to initiate treatment activities. In this regard, it was useful to have a service coordinator who was also a child welfare supervisor with knowledge and experience in both the investigative and treatment elements of child abuse. In terms of a smooth and immediate service response, having the service coordinator placed in the child welfare agency ensured that all cases were identified as soon as disclosures were made and that immediate contact could be initiated by child-welfare abuse investigators. An important aspect in linking to treatment (through the securing of case managers) was the ongoing contact the service coordinator maintained with potential treatment providers through the community treatment committee. However, aspects of this interagency collaboration represented the 'down side' of having a child welfare supervisor function as the service coordinator. Often workers from other community agencies felt they were 'cogs in a child welfare machine.' The coordinated service system might have proceeded more smoothly if the service coordinator's position had been filled by a person seconded from the child welfare agency, but who was seen to be fulfilling an independent service role jointly funded by the provincial government's Department of Family Services (responsible for child welfare), Department of Health (responsible for community mental health services), and Department of Justice (responsible for the courts and judicial proceedings).

Much responsibility for the maintenance of a collaborative service approach during the treatment phase rests in the hands of the individual case managers. This can be both a strength and a weakness in the coordinated model. Its strength is that each case has someone who is responsible for tracking the progress of the case and ensuring that services are being provided according to a systemic plan. Its weakness lies in the energy of each case manager and his or her committment to promote a service system that is in the best interest of the client. Interdisciplinary boundaries can be most sensitive when decisions are made with respect to service delivery. It was important in our experience to ensure that clinicians felt they controlled the 'how' of the process of therapy. That is, the case manager could ensure that participants in a treatment team met their commitments to deliver service, but could not tell them how to do it.

An important issue that emerged here involved the availability of ongoing practice supervision. Workers in this project often expressed frustration that more clinical supervision was not available to them. While this is not unusual, particularly for those providing therapy in rural settings, it did emerge as an area of important need in our project. Perhaps this is one of the inherent deficiencies in an interagency collaborative treatment system. When treatment teams are centralized in one agency or facility, it is more straight-forward to establish lines of supervisory authority. In interagency systems a great deal can be gained from peer review and peer consultation. However, the case-by-case supervision within a service sector (such as child welfare or community mental health) must be respected and each service sector encouraged to secure its own clinical supervision resources.

It was during the treatment phase that it was most important to maintain high interdisciplinary congruence with respect to a shared ideology of treatment. Because the bulk of the treatment providers shared a 'family systems view' of intervention, collaborative case planning was more readily achieved. Because the bulk of treatment providers appreciated the need for sequential and multi-modal therapies (e.g., individual counselling, group sessions, dyadic interventions, and family therapy), there were few professional skirmishes over treatment plans. The challenge seemed less that of putting together a shared strategy of intervention than in finding the necessary basic clinical resources needed to help abused children and their family adequately.

It is beyond the scope of this book to comment in detail on how readily our model of coordinated services could be applied in more densely populated urban communities. We would anticipate that 'consensus building,' which is the essence of coordinated systems, will be more difficult because interagency 'program territorial concerns' would likely be more pronounced and there would be more participating professionals embracing a wider range of service beliefs and ideologies. Because of 'the large number of competitive service providers' and the greater 'complexity of delivery systems,' integrative service links will be more difficult to create in urban settings than in rural ones (Morrill 1976, p. 54). However we would speculate that the key service positions that have been identified in this rural project (i.e., service coordinator, case manager, parent support worker) will have immediate relevancy to those responding to child sexual abuse in cities.

It is important to recognize that the coordinated model will inherently mean periods of heightened anxiety and stress in professionals as the system is being created and implemented. Individual professionals do see immediate benefits using the collaborative approach in rural locales. They do value the emotional and practical support it can bring from their fellow professionals, and appreciate the potential learning and professional growth offered by close collaboration with other caregivers. However, there is heightened stress associated with being within the close scrutiny of others as they become accountable beyond the reach of their home agency for the quality of their professional practice. In this regard, the community treatment committee is a vital aspect of the model because it provides system participants with a structured setting in which to voice their concerns, attitudes, and perceptions concerning the highs and lows of their collaborative efforts in dealing with child sexual abuse.

One of the most challenging aspects of our project was the need to integrate research requirements with practice priorities. Doing applied research in the area of child sexual abuse is not for the faint of heart. One is dealing with highly reactive clients who for the most part do not wish to divulge information about their thoughts, feelings, or personal situations at a time when they are under stress and face hazardous family and community circumstances. At the same time, one is often dealing with 'reactive' professionals as well; that is, professionals who feel the power of the social circumstance in which they must intervene, and who often feel overwhelmed by the huge and complex service demands they are facing. In such circumstances, one must proceed with tact, diplomacy, and carefully realistic expectations concerning the gathering of research information.

This project was further limited by the small numbers of cases that provided its database for statistical analyses. With the size of sample available there was limited power in statistical analyses. This meant that substantially large differences were required to achieve statistical significance, and there was a conservative estimate of change between pre-treatment and post-treatment scores. However, comprehensive quantitative information was collected on each case under study, and qualitative analyses were employed to supplement and extend quantitative findings. With two well-matched comparison service systems, differences between test and comparison areas were less likely to be biased by extraneous client or community factors.

From a clinical evaluation perspective, there was high substantive significance (Smith 1976) to the findings in psychological measures, particularly when these were verified on a case-by-case clinical review. Projects such as this one cannot definitively prove complex research hypotheses. However, there was high consistency in the wide range of information collected, which served to support the contention that the coordinated service model was of greater benefit to rural clients than the traditional, individualized, agency service response.

One of the long-term benefits of the coordinated service approach that we could not evaluate over the term of our project, but that we anticipate will be a positive result of this approach, is the reduced numbers of unsubstantiated disclosures – particularly as these occur in older children. It does seem that there is a 'child sexual abuse accommodation syndrome' (Summit 1983) in which strong forces within the family and community steer children into retracting their allegations of sexual abuse. Certainly, fragmented and confusing investigative procedures by police and child welfare workers only serve to exacerbate the victim's sense of personal isolation from others and her or his perception of disbelief in others.

Older children are more aware of the price they will pay when they make an allegation of sexual abuse. Many of these children, who have experienced the intrusion of professionals in the life of their family, know that the extended disruption the investigative and court procedures will introduce into their lives is not worth its situational and emotional cost. Many children have learned that it is best to deny that abuse is occurring, and to seek alternative measures to secure safety for themselves from sexual assault within their families. We anticipate that thoughtful and coordinated services, those that span the investigation and treatment of child sexual abuse, will remedy these negative service experiences that further victimize sexually abused children.

We hope we will contribute, through this project, not only to the further development of coordinated service systems for improved professional responses to situations of intrafamilial child sexual abuse in rural locales, but also to what might be continued research explorations in this difficult study area. If services are to be improved, it is our belief that there needs to be more systematic record keeping as well as standardized approaches in assessing the impact of services. It seems that overextended practitioners, who are contending with large caseloads of complex sexual abuse situations, are by necessity careful in their management of their work time. It is understandable that they wish to collect only information that is directly relevant to their work, that is required in the mandated activities they must perform for the courts or for their agencies, and that is of a scope that will not put an unnecessary strain on their personal relationship with their troubled clients. We hope that the service information protocols that have emerged from this experience in several rural communities will be useful to those wishing to monitor the impact of their services and to better understand the social and psychological circumstances of those they wish to assist.

This project attempted to explicate and evaluate an integrated service response to a highly challenging social, legal, and behavioural problem. That is, to advance understanding of how to design and implement coordinated community services that respond to child sexual abuse. On the basis of this experience, we would conclude that the coordinated model of service delivery has the potential to substantially reduce 'institutional trauma' – the trauma experienced by children and family members when professional caregivers intrude into their lives during the investigation and early treatment of intrafamilial child sexual abuse. It is our hope that the knowledge gained from this project will serve to improve the quality of services, particularly in rural Canadian communities, for sexually abused children and their family members.

References

Achenbach, T.M., & McConaughy, S.H. (1987). Empirically based assessment of child and adolescent psychopathology. Newbury Park, CA: Sage.

Achenbach, T.M. & Edelbrock, C. (1983). *Manual for the child behavior checklist
and revised child behavior profile*. Burlington: University of Vermont Department of Psychiatry.

Adams-Tucker, C. (1982). Proximate effects of sexual abuse in childhood: A
report on 28 children. *American Journal of Psychiatry, 139* (10), 1252–1256.

Adkins, E., Trute, B., MacDonald, G., McCannell, K., Herbert, C., Hill, E.,
& Scuse, D. (1991). Child sexual abuse in rural community settings: The
implementation and evaluation of a coordinated service model. Demon-
stration project final report: National Welfare Grants Project #4556, 1-19.
(Available from Child and Family Services Research Group, Faculty of
Social Work, University of Manitoba, Winnipeg R3T 2N2, Canada.)

Attias, R., & Goodwin, J. (1985). Knowledge and management strategies in
incest cases: A survey of physicians, psychologists and family counsellors. *Child Abuse and Neglect, 9,* 527–533.

Attkisson, C.C., & Zwick, R. (1982). The client satisfaction questionnaire.
Evaluation and Program Planning, 5, 233–237.

Badgley, R. (Chair). (1984). *Report of the committee on sexual violence against children and youths*. Ottawa: Government of Canada, Department of Justice
and Department of National Health and Welfare.

Bagarozzi, D. (1982). The family therapist's role in treating families in rural
areas. *Journal of Marital and Family Therapy, 8* (2), 51–58.

Baglow, L.J. (1990). A multidimensional model for treatment of child abuse:
A framework for cooperation. *Child Abuse and Neglect, 14,* 387–395.

Beck, A.T., & Beck, R.W. (1972). Screening depressed patients in family practice: A rapid technique. *Postgraduate Medicine, 52*, 233–237.

Bedford, A. (1983). Aspects of child abuse in Britain. In N. Ebling & D. Hill (Eds.), *Child abuse and neglect: A guide with case studies for treating the child and the family.* Boston: John Wright.

Benjamin, J. (1981). Child abuse and the interdisciplinary team: Panacea or problem' In H.H. Irving (Ed.), *Family law: An interdisciplinary perspective.* Toronto: Carswell.

Berliner, L. (1988). In D. Hechler (Ed.) *The battle and the backlash: The child sexual abuse war.* Lexington, MA: Lexington Books.

Berry, B., & Davis, A.E. (1978), Community mental health ideology: A problematic model for rural areas. *American Journal Orthopsychiatry, 48*, 673–679.

Brockopp, G.W. (1973). Crisis intervention: Theory, process and practice. *Crisis Intervention and Counselling by Telephone: Chapter 6.* Springfield, IL: Charles C. Thomas.

Bronfenbrenner, U. (1979). *The ecology of human development: Experiments by nature and design.* Cambridge, MA: Harvard University Press.

Butler, S. (1978). *Conspiracy of silence: The trauma of incest.* Volcano, CA: Volcano Press.

Byerly, C.M. (1985). Mother survival in the incestuous family. *Sexual Coercion and Assault, 1* (1), 11–13.

Byles, J.A. (1985). Problems in inter-agency collaboration: Lessons from a project that failed. *Child Abuse and Neglect, 9*, 549–554.

Caplan, G. (1964). *Principles of preventive psychiatry.* New York: Basic Books.

Carl, D., & Jurkovic, G.J. (1983). Agency triangles: Problems in agency-family relationships. *Family Process, 22*, 441–451.

Carroll, C. (1978). The protective worker's role in treatment. In B. Schmitt (Ed.), *The child protection team handbook: The multidisciplinary approach to managing child abuse and neglect* (p.221). New York: Garland.

Cohen, T. (1983). The incestuous family re-visited. *Social Casework, 64* (3),154–161.

Conte, J.R. (1984). Progress in treating the sexual abuse of children. *Social Work*, 258–263.

Cook, T.D., & Campbell, D.T. (1979). *Quasi-experimentation design and analysis issues for field settings.* Skokie, IL: Rand McNally.

Craft, J.L., & Clarkson, C.D. (1985). Case disposition recommendations of attorneys and social workers in child abuse investigations. *Child Abuse and Neglect, 9*, 165–174.

Dale, P., & Davies, M. (1985). A model of intervention in child-abusing families: A wider systems view. *Child Abuse and Neglect, 9,* 449–455.

Dale, P., Davies, M., Morrison, T., & Waters, J. (1986). *Dangerous families: Assessment and treatment of child abuse.* London: Tavistock.

Dale, P., Waters, J., Davies, M., Roberts, W., & Morrison, T. (1986). The towers of silence: Creative and destructive issues for therapeutic teams dealing with sexual abuse. *Journal of Family Therapy, 8* (1), 1–25.

Dietz, C.A., & Craft, J.L. (1980, December). Family dynamics of incest: A new perspective. *Social Casework: The Journal of Contemporary Social Work,* 602–609.

Edgerton, J.W., & Bentz, W.K. (1969). Attitudes and opinions of rural people about mental illness and program services. *American Journal of Public Health, 59,* 470–477.

Elbow, M., & Mayfield, J. (1991, February). Mothers of incest victims: Villains, victims or protectors? *Families in Society: The Journal of Contemporary Human Services,* 78–86.

Ellis, E. (1989). Written communication to G. Macdonald.

Everson, M.D., Hunter, W.M., Runyon, D.K., Edelsohn, G.A., & Coulter, M.L. (1989). Maternal support following disclosure of incest. *American Journal of Orthopsychiatry, 59* (2), 197–207.

Faller, K.C. (1989). Why sexual abuse? An exploration of the intergenerational hypothesis. *Child Abuse and Neglect, 13,* 543–548.

– (1988). Decision making in cases of intrafamilial child sexual abuse. *American Journal Orthopsychiatry, 58* (1), 121–128.

Fauber, R., Forehand, R., Long, N., Burke, M., & Faust, J. (1987). The relationship of young adolescent Children's Depression Inventory (CDI) scores to their social and cognitive functioning. *Journal of Psychopathology and Behavioral Assessment, 9* (2), 161–172.

Finkelhor, D. (1984). *Child sexual abuse: New theory and research.* New York: The Free Press.

Finkelhor, D., Gomes-Schwartz, B., & Horowitz, J. (1982, 2 December). Agency management of sexual abuse: Responses and attitudes from a survey of Boston professionals. Paper presented to the Massachusetts Psychological Association, Boston, MA.

Fletcher, L. (1982). Battered professionals. In K. Oates (Ed.), *Child abuse: A community concern.* Secaucus, N.J.: Citadel Press.

Friedrich, W.N. (1990). *Psychotherapy of sexually abused children and their families.* New York: Norton.

Frosh, S. (1988). No man's land? The role of men working with sexually abused children. *British Journal of Guidance and Counselling, 16* (3), 1–10.

Fryer, G.E., Poland, J.E., Bross, D.C., & Krugman, R.D. (1988) The child protective social worker: A profile of needs, attitudes and utilization of professional resources. *Child Abuse and Neglect, 12,* 481–490.

Furniss, T. (1983). Mutual influence and interlocking professional–family process in the treatment of child sexual abuse and incest. *Child Abuse and Neglect, 7,* 207–223.

– (1991). *The multi-professional handbook of child sexual abuse: Integrated management, therapy and legal interventions.* London: Routledge.

Gelinas, D.J. (1983). The persisting negative effects of incest. *Psychiatry, 46,* 312–332.

– (1986). Unexpected resources in treating incest families. In M.A. Karpel (Ed.) *Family Resources* Chapter 11. New York: Guilford Press.

Giaretto, H. (1986). *A comprehensive child sexual abuse treatment programme.* Secaucus, NJ: Citadel Press.

– (1982). *Treatment of child sexual abuse: A treatment and training manual.* Palo Alto, CA: Science and Behavior Books.

– (1976, July/August). The treatment of father-daughter incest: A psychosocial approach. *Children Today.*

Golan, N. (1978). *Treatment in crisis situations.* New York: The Free Press.

Gottman, J.M., & Leiblum, S.R. (1974). *How to do psychotherapy and how to evaluate it.* New York: Holt, Rinehart and Winston.

Gurian, H. (1971). A decade in rural psychiatry. *Hospital and Community Psychiatry,* 40–42.

Hartman, A., & Laird, J. (1983). *Family-centered social work practice.* New York: The Free Press.

Health Promotions Branch, Health Services Directorate, Health and Welfare Canada (1989). *Health care related to abuse, assault, neglect: Family violence guidelines* (pp. 35–38). Ottawa, Canada.

Hechler, D., (1988). *The battle and the backlash.* Lexington, MA: Lexington Books.

Heger, A., & Summit, R. (1981, 8 June). Society called blind to child abuse. *The Toronto Globe and Mail,* p. 3.

Helfer, R.E., & Schmidt, R. (1976). The community based child abuse and neglect program. In R.E. Helfer and C.H. Kempe (Eds.), *Child abuse and neglect: The family and the community,* Chapter 13. Cambridge, MA: Balinger.

Herbert, C., Grams, G., & Trute, B. (1986). B.C.: Pacific Coast Family Therapy Training Association.

Herman, J. (1981). Father-daughter incest. *Professional Psychology, 1* (1).

Herman, J., & Hirschman, L. (1977). Father-daughter incest. *Signs, 2* (4), 735–756.

Hirsch, B.J. (1980). Natural support systems and coping with major life changes. *American Journal of Community Psychology, 8*, 159–172.

Hobbs, C.J., & Wynne, J.M. (1986, 4 October). Buggery in childhood: A common syndrome of child abuse. *The Lancet*, 792–796.

Hochstadt, N.J., & Harwick, N.J. (1985). How effective is the multidisciplinary approach? A follow-up study. *Child Abuse and Neglect, 9*, 365–372.

Horowitz, M.J., Wilner, N., & Alvarez, W. (1979). Impact of event scale: A measure of subjective stress. *Psychological Medicine, 41*, 209–218.

Hudson, W.W., (1982). *The clinical measurement package: A field manual.* Chicago: Dorsey Press.

Huessy, H.R. (1969). Rural models. In L. Bellak and H. Barton (Eds.), *Progress in Community Mental Health*, Vol. 2. New York: Grune and Stratton, 199–220.

Imber-Black, E. (1991). A family-larger-system perspective. In A.S. Gurman & D.P. Kniskern (Eds.), *Handbook of Family Therapy*, Vol. 2, Chapter 19. New York: Brunner/Mazel.

Imber Coppersmith, E. (1982). The family and public service systems: An assessment method. In B. Keeny (Ed.), *Diagnosis and assessment in family therapy.* Rockville, MD: Aspen Systems.

Jackson, T.L., & Sandberg, G. (1985). Attribution of incest blame among rural attorneys and judges, *Women and Therapy, 4*, 39–57.

James B., & Nasjleti, M. (1983). *Treating sexually abused children and their families,* Palo Alto, CA: Consulting Psychologist Press.

Kazdin, A.E., & Wilson, G.T. (1978). Criteria for evaluating psychotherapy. *Archives of General Psychiatry, 35*, 407–416.

Kelley, S.J. (1990). Responsibilities and management strategies in child sexual abuse: A comparison of child protective workers, nurses and police officers. *Child Welfare, 6* (1), 4–51.

Kinder Matthews, J., Raymaker, J., & Speltz, K. (1991). Effects of reunification on sexually abusive families. In M.Q. Patton (Ed.), *Family Sexual Abuse: Frontline Research and Evaluation*, Chapter 10. Newbury Park: Sage.

Kroth, J.A. (1979). *Child sexual abuse: Analysis of family therapy approach.* Springfield, IL: Charles C. Thomas.

Land, H.M. (1986). Child abuse: Differential diagnosis, differential treatment. *Child Welfare, 65*(1), 33–44.

Larson, N., & Maddock, J. (1986). Structural and functional variables in incest family systems: Implications for assessment and treatment. *Journal of Psychotherapy and the Family, 2* (2), 27–44.

– (1989). Workshop held in Portage la Prairie, Manitoba, 24–26 June.

Levitt, C.J., Owen, G., & Truchsess, J. (1991). Families after sexual abuse: What helps? What is needed? In M.Q. Patton (Ed.), *Family sexual abuse: Frontline research and evaluation*, Chapter 3. Newbury Park: Sage.

Litwak, E., & Hylton, L.F. (1962). Interorganizational analysis: A hypothesis on coordinating agencies. *Administrative Sciences Quarterly, 6*, 395–420.

MacFarlane, K., & Bulkley, J. (1982, Fall/Winter). Treating child sexual abuse: An overview of current program models. *Journal of Social Work and Human Sexuality, Special Double Issue: Social Work and Child Sexual Abuse, 1,* 69-93.

Madanes, C. (1990). *Sex, Love and Violence.* New York: W.W. Norton.

McCannell Saulnier, K. (1984). Social Networks and the transition to motherhood: A longitudinal analysis. PhD Dissertation. University of Manitoba.

McCannell Saulnier, K., & Rowland, C. (1985, October). Missing links: An empirical investigation of network variables in high-risk families. *Family Relations, 34,* 557-560.

Martin, M.J. (1992). Child sexual abuse: Preventing continued victimization by the criminal justice system and associated agencies. *Family Relations, 41,* 330-333.

Meddin, B.J, & Hansen, I. (1985). The services provided during a child abuse and/or neglect case investigation and the barriers that exist to service provision. *Child Abuse and Neglect, 9,* 175-182.

Morrill, W.A. (1976). Services integration and the Department of Health, Education and Welfare, *Evaluation, 3* (1-2), 53-55.

Oritt, E.J., Paul S.C., & Behrman, J.A. (1985). The perceived social support inventory. *American Journal of Community Psychology, 13,* 565-582.

Rapoport, L. (1962). The state of crisis: Some theoretical considerations. *Social Service Review, 32* (2), 211-217.

Rivera, M. (1988). Social systems intervention in families of victims of child sexual abuse. *Canadian Journal of Community Mental Health, 7* (1).

Rogers, R. (1990, June). *Reaching for solutions.* Ottawa: National Clearing-house on Family Violence in Canada, Health and Welfare Canada.

Rowe, D.C., & Plomin, R. (1977). Temperament in early childhood. *Journal of Personality Assessment, 4* (2), 150-156.

Russell, D. (1984). The prevalence and seriousness of incestuous abuse: Stepfathers vs. biological fathers. *Child Abuse and Neglect, 8,* 15-22.

Russell, D., Peplau, L.A., & Cutrona, C.E. (1980). The revised UCLA Loneliness Scale: Concurrent and discriminant validity evidence. *Journal of Personality and Social Psychology, 3* (3), 472-480.

Rutter, M. (1975). *Helping Troubled Children.* Markham: Penguin Education.

Sas, L. (Principal Investigator) (1991). *Reducing the system-induced trauma for child sexual abuse victims through court preparation, assessment and follow-up.* Final Report, National Welfare Grants, Health and Welfare Canada, Project #4555-1-125.

Saunders, E. (1988) A comparative study of attitudes toward child sexual abuse among social work and judicial system professionals. *Child Abuse and Neglect, 12,* 83–90.

Schultz, L. (1973). The child sex victim: Social, psychological and legal perspectives. *Child Welfare, 52,* 147–157.

Sefcik, T.R., & Ormsby N.J. (1978). Establishing a rural child abuse/neglect treatment program. *Child Welfare, 57* (3), 187–195.

Server, J.C., & Janzen, C. (1982). Contraindications to reconstitution of sexually abusive families. *Child Welfare, 5,* 279–288.

Sgroi, S.M. (Ed.) (1982). *Handbook of clinical intervention in child sexual abuse.* Lexington, MA: Lexington Books.

Sgroi, S.M., & Dana, N.T. (1982). Individual and group treatment of mothers of incest victims. In S.M. Sgroi (Ed.), *Handbook of clinical intervention in child sexual abuse,* Lexington, MA: Lexington Books.

Skinner, H.A., Steinhauer, P.D., & Santa-Barbara, J. (1983). The family assessment measure. *Canadian Journal of Community Mental Health, 2* (2), 91–105.

Smith, L. (1976). A general model of crisis intervention. *Clinical Social Work Journal, 4* (3), 162–171.

Strahan, R., & Gerbasi, K.C. (1972). Short, homogeneous versions and the Marlow-Crowne Social Desirability Scale. *Journal of Clinical Psychology, 28,* 191–193.

Summit, R.C. (1983). The child sexual abuse accommodation syndrome. *Child Abuse and Neglect, 7,* 177–193.

Thorman, G. (1983). *Incestuous families.* Springfield, IL: Charles C. Thomas.

Tranel, N. (1970). Rural program development. In H. Grunebaum (Ed.), *The practice of community mental health,* Boston: Little, Brown, 413–438.

Trepper, T.S. (1986). The apology session. In T.S. Trepper and M.J. Barrett (Eds.), *Treating Incest: A multiple systems perspective.,* Binghamton, NY: Haworth Press.

– (1989). Intrafamily child sexual abuse. In C.R. Figley (Ed.), *Treating stress in families,* Chapter 7. New York: Brunner/Mazel.

Trepper, T.S., & Barrett, M.J. (1986), Vulnerability to incest: A framework for assessment. In T.S. Trepper & M.J. Barrett (Eds.), *Treating incest: A multiple systems perspective.* Binghamton, NY: The Haworth Press.

Trute, B. (1983). Human factors inherent in system survival. In E.M. Bennett & B. Trute, *Mental Health Information Systems: Problems and Prospects,* Chapter 4. New York: Edwin Mellen Press.

Trute, B., Adkins, E., & MacDonald, G. (1992). Professional attitudes regarding the sexual abuse of children: Comparing police, child welfare and community mental health. *Child Abuse and Neglect, 16, 359–368.*

Trute, B., Tefft, B., & Scuse, D. (1985). *Human service information systems.* New York: Edwin Mellen Press.

Tucker, D.J. (1979). *Coordination in the social services sector: The facts of life!* Hamilton: The School of Social Work, McMaster University.

Wilk, R., & McCarthy, C. (1986, January). Intervention in child sexual abuse: A survey of attitudes. *Social Casework: The Journal of Contemporary Social Work.*

Woodard, L., & Woodard, B. (1983). The larger system in the treatment of incest. *Journal of Strategic and Systemic Therapies, 2,* 28–37.

Zilberg, N.J., Weiss, D.S., & Horowitz, M.J. (1982). Impact of event scale: A cross-validation study and some empirical evidence supporting a conceptual model of stress response syndromes. *Journal of Consulting and Clinical Psychology, 50* (3), 407–414.

Author Index

Subject Index